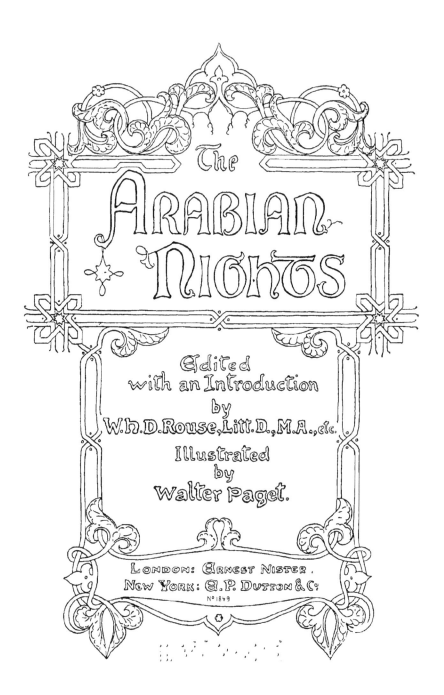

The
ARABIAN
NIGHTS

Edited
with an Introduction
by
W.h.D.Rouse,Litt.D.,M.A.,etc.

Illustrated
by
Walter Paget.

LONDON: ERNEST NISTER.
NEW YORK: E.P. DUTTON & C.
Nº 1849

CONTENTS.

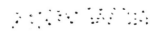

INTRODUCTION.

THE book of the Arabian Nights' Entertainment, or, more properly, The Thousand and One Nights, is not very ancient in its present shape The book was first made known in the West by Antoine Galland, who in 1704 published a paraphrase in French of a manuscript which came into his hands This manuscript, which was in existence in 1548, is not very much earlier than that date; and the internal evidence of the tales, the atmosphere and setting, points to a date not earlier than 1450 for their compilation in this form. While, however, the atmosphere is Moslem and the setting or local colour points to Egypt in the 14th to 16th centuries, the tales themselves point to Arabia, and in particular to the heyday of Bagdad with the Caliph Haroun al Reschid. Some of the tales have a historical basis, some are Persian or Indian; others are folk-tales or older than the hills, there are not a few repetitions. All this evidence indicates that the work is a compilation based on one or more older collections. and incorporating a number of stray legends and stories, one of the collections incorporated being Arabian and the final compilation having been made in Egypt somewhere about 1500.

Galland's French paraphrase is a charming work, but it was meant as a children's story book and has no pretentions to scholarly accuracy. it is very much shortened and selects only a part of the material. Two of the most famous stories, Aladdin and Ali Baba, together with others, did not proceed from this collection of the Nights at all, but from another manuscript, which was afterwards identified by Doctor Zotenberg in Paris Upon Galland's paraphrase are based a number of other selections and adaptations Early in the 19th century Jonathan Scott produced an English revision or paraphrase selected from the contents of a manuscript in the possession of Edward Wortley Montague (1811, reprinted later) This also contains only a small part of the original. In 1839, E W. Lane made an independent English translation from an abbreviated version of the Arabic text, which has been several times reprinted and represents what the English reader regards as the Arabian Nights' Entertainment. He, like the rest, selected, abbreviated

countries where books are few, the hearing of stories is the spice
of life, lifting all above their own sordid surroundings, giving
happiness to those in trouble and hope to all   The following
description from a traveller who knew the Arabs well will
illustrate this

"The fondness of an Arab for the traditional history of the
most distinguisht actions of their remote ancestors is proverbial.
professed story-tellers are ever the appendages of men of rank.
It is a great exercise of genius, and a peculiar gift, held in
high estimation among them.   They have a quickness and clear-
ness of delivery, with a perfect command of words, surprising
to a European ear; they never hesitate, are never at a loss,
their descriptions are highly poetical, and their relations exempli-
fied by figure and metaphor, the most striking and appropriate,
their extempore songs are also full of fire, and possess many
beautiful and happy similes

"Arab songs go to the heart, and greatly excite the passions
I have seen a circle of Arabs straining their eyes with fixed
attention one moment, and bursting with loud laughter. at the
next, melting into tears, and clasping their hands in all the
ecstasy of grief and sympathy "—Denham's *Travels in Africa*.

From stories men gain their history and geography, their
science and their rules of life ; they include for unlettered races
their education and their religion   I venture to hope that those
who may procure this book for their children will use it in the
good old way and tell the stories by word of mouth, or at least
read them aloud   Few memories are so lasting as those of the
stories which we heard told or read to us in childhood, and to
many the memory of a nurse or foster mother is among their
dearest thoughts, bringing gratitude for the new worlds of imagi-
nation which they have opened up, never to be obliterated
throughout the struggles of after life

W H D Rouse

THE MERCHANT AND THE GENIE.

THERE was once a merchant who possessed much
property in lands, goods, and money, and had
a great number of clerks, factors, and slaves. He
was obliged from time to time to take business
journeys, and on one occasion he took horse, and
carried with him a wallet containing biscuits and
dates, because he had a great desert to pass over,
where he could procure no sort of provisions. He
arrived without accident at the end of his journey,
and, having despatched his affairs, took horse again
in order to return home.

The fourth day of his journey he turned out of
the road to rest for a while beneath some trees.

He found a fountain near at hand, so, tying his horse
to the branch of a tree, he seated himself beside
the fountain and took some biscuits and dates from
his wallet.

As he ate his dates he threw the stones carelessly in different directions; then, having finished
his repast, being a good Mussulman, he washed his
hands, face, and feet, and said his prayers.

Before he had finished he saw a genie, white
with age and of enormous size, advancing towards
him with a scimitar in his hand. He spoke to him
in a terrible voice, bidding him "Rise, that I may
kill you with this scimitar, as you have killed
my son."

"How could I kill your son?" exclaimed the
merchant, "I never knew, never saw him."

"Did you not sit down when you came hither?"
demanded the genie, "and did you not take dates
out of your wallet, and as you ate them did you
not throw the stones about in different directions?"

"I did all that you say," answered the merchant;
"I cannot deny it."

"If it be so," reasoned the genie, "I tell you
that you have killed my son: and in this manner.
When you were throwing the stones about, my son
was passing by and you threw one into his eye,
which killed him; therefore I must kill you."

"Ah! my Lord! pardon me!" exclaimed the
merchant

"No pardon, no mercy," exclaimed the genie. "Is it not just to kill him that has killed another?"

"I agree it is," replied the merchant, "but if I killed your son it was unknown to me, and I did it innocently; I beg you therefore to pardon me, and suffer me to live."

But as the genie persisted in his resolution the merchant begged that he might be granted a year's respite in which to return home, bid farewell to his wife and children, and settle his business affairs.

"Do you take heaven to witness," cried the genie, "that this day twelvemonth you will return to this spot?"

"I do," answered the merchant, whereupon the genie left him and disappeared

The merchant then hastened to return home and acquaint his family with the sorrowful intelligence. There was great lamentation made, and his wife and children wept bitterly, the merchant himself mingling his tears with theirs; but notwithstanding this he did not neglect to set his affairs in order, and at the end of the twelvemonth he bade his family adieu and set out upon his journey to the appointed spot.

He reached the fountain, alighted from his horse, and seated himself upon the ground.

He had not been there long when he saw an old man, leading a hind, approaching.

"Brother," said the old man, "why are you

come to this desert place, which is the resort of an evil spirit?"

The merchant satisfied his curiosity and related to him the adventure which obliged him to be there. The old man listened with astonishment and when he had finished exclaimed "I will remain, Brother, and be a witness of your interview with the genie"

They conversed together for a short time and then perceived another old man coming towards them, followed by two black dogs.

After they had saluted one another, he asked them what they did in that place. The old man with the hind told him the adventure of the merchant and the genie, and all that had passed between them, and the second old man resolved also to remain and witness the issue of the meeting.

They had seriously begun to converse together when they perceived a thick vapour, like a cloud of dust raised by a whirlwind, advancing towards them, and out of the vapour appeared the genie, having a scimitar in his hand

Taking the merchant by the arm, he said "Rise, that I may kill you as you killed my son."

When the old man who led the hind saw the genie lay hold of the merchant and about to kill him, he threw himself at the feet of the monster and said "Prince of Genies, I most humbly request you to suspend your anger, and do me the favour to hear me I will tell you the history of my life, and of

"Brother," said the old man, "why are you come to this desert place?"

the hind you see; and if you think it more wonderful and surprising than the adventure of the merchant,
I hope you will pardon the unfortunate man one
half of his offence."

The genie after deliberating a short time on
the proposal finally agreed to it

So the old man began his story "This hind,"
said he, "is my cousin; nay, what is more, my wife.
She was very young when I married her, and after
living together twenty years and having no children,
I took a second wife, a slave. This slave wife
presented me with a son, and my wife, being jealous,
hated both mother and son; but concealed her
aversion so well that I knew nothing of it till it
was too late.

"When my son was grown to a youth I was
obliged to undertake a long journey Before I went
I recommended to my wife, of whom I had no
mistrust, the slave and her son, and prayed her to
take care of them during my absence, which was to
be for a whole year.

"But, having studied magic, she succeeded by
her enchantments in changing my son into a calf
and his mother into a cow.

"At my return I enquired for mother and child.

"'Your slave,' said she, 'is dead; and as for your
son, I know not what has become of him I have
not seen him these two months.'

"Eight months passed and my son did not return,

and, it being the feast of the great Sacrifice, I bade my herdsman bring me a fat cow to sacrifice.

"He accordingly brought me one, and having bound her I was about to make the sacrifice, but she bellowed so piteously, tears falling from her eyes, that I could not bring myself to give her the blow; but delivered her to my herdsman, who took her away and slaughtered her. But when he came to skin her he found her to be nothing but skin and bone.

"'Take her yourself,' I said, 'and dispose of her in alms, or in any way you please, and if you have a fat calf, bring it me in her stead.'

"He returned shortly with a fat calf, and though I knew not the calf was my son, yet I could not forbear being moved at the sight of him. On his part, as soon as he beheld me, he made so great an effort to come near me, that he broke his cord and threw himself at my feet as if conjuring me not to be so cruel as to take his life.

"I felt a tender pity for him, which interested me on his behalf, and I bade the herdsman take the calf home and bring me another in his stead

"Although my wife urged me again and again to make the sacrifice, I could not bring myself to do so, and the herdsman led him away The following morning the herdsman desired to speak with me alone.

"'I come,' said he, 'to communicate to you a

piece of intelligence for which I hope you will return
me thanks. I have a daughter that has some skill
in magic. Yesterday when I led the calf home I
perceived she laughed when she saw him, and in a
moment after fell a-weeping. I asked her why
she acted two such opposite parts at one and the

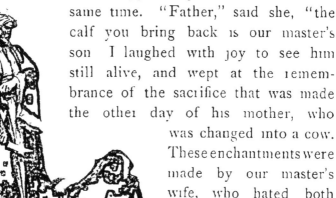

same time. "Father," said she, "the
calf you bring back is our master's
son I laughed with joy to see him
still alive, and wept at the remem-
brance of the sacrifice that was made
the other day of his mother, who
was changed into a cow.
These enchantments were
made by our master's
wife, who hated both
mother and son."

"On hearing these
words I hastened to the
house of my herdsman
and asked his daughter

*He broke his cord and threw
himself at my feet.*

if she were able to restore my son to his former
shape.

"She answered me, smiling, 'You are our master,
and I well know what I owe to you, but I cannot
restore your son to his former shape, except on two
conditions the first is, that you give him to me for
my husband, and the second, that you allow me to
punish the person who changed him into a calf.'

"Having agreed to both these conditions, the damsel took a vessel full of water, pronounced words over it that I did not understand, and, addressing herself to the calf, exclaimed 'O calf, if thou wast born a calf, continue in that form; but if thou be a man, and art changed into a calf by enchantment, return to thy natural shape.'

"As she spoke, she threw water upon him, and in an instant he recovered his natural form.

"We embraced each other tenderly, and I then addressed him in these words 'I doubt not but in acknowledgment to your deliverer you will consent to make her your wife, as I have promised.'

"He consented joyfully, but before they were married she changed my wife into a hind, and this is she whom you see.

"This is the history of myself and this hind. Is it not one of the most wonderful and surprising?"

"I admit it is," said the genie, "and on that account forgive the merchant one half of his crime."

When the first old man had finished his story, the second, who led the two black dogs, addressed the genie and said:—

"I am going to tell you what happened to me, and these two black dogs you see by me, and I am certain you will say that my story is yet more surprising than that which you have just heard. But when I have done this, I hope you will be pleased to pardon the merchant another half of his offence"

"I will," replied the genie, "provided your story surpass that of the hind."

Then the second old man began

"Great Prince of Genies, you must know that we are three brothers, the two black dogs and myself. Our father, when he died, left each of us one thousand sequins. With that sum we all became merchants. A little time after we opened shop, my eldest brother, one of these two dogs, resolved to travel and trade in foreign countries With this view he sold his estate, and bought goods suited to the trade he intended to follow

"He went away and was absent a whole year. At the expiration of this time, a poor man who I thought had come to ask alms presented himself before me in my shop.

"'Is it possible you do not know me?' he cried, and upon this I looked at him narrowly and recognised him. 'Ah, brother,' cried I, embracing him, 'how could I know you in this condition?' I made him come into my house, and having questioned him concerning his misfortunes, I found that he had lost all his goods and money through unfortunate trading.

"I immediately shut up my shop and, taking him to a bath, gave him the best clothes I had. Finding, on examining my books, that I had doubled my stock, that is to say, that I was worth two thousand sequins, I gave him one-half, 'With that,' said I,

you may make up your loss.' He joyfully accepted
the present, and having repaired his fortunes, we
lived together as before.

"Some time after, my second brother, who is the
other of these two dogs, also sold his estate.

"His elder brother and myself did all we could
to divert him from his purpose, but without effect.
He disposed of it, and with the money bought such
goods as were suitable to the trade which he
designed to follow. He joined a caravan and departed. At the end of the year he returned in the
same condition as my other brother. Having myself
by this time gained another thousand sequins, I made
him a present of them. With this sum he furnished
his shop, and continued his trade

"Some time after, one of my brothers came to
me to propose that I should join them in a trading
voyage· I immediately declined 'You have travelled,' said I, 'and what have you gained by it'
Who can assure me that I shall be more successful
than you have been.' In vain they urged me, for I
constantly refused, but after having resisted their
solicitation five whole years, they importuned me so
much, that at last they overcame my resolution.

"When, however, the time arrived that we were
to make preparations for our voyage, to buy the
goods necessary to the undertaking, I found they had
spent all, and had not one dirrim left of the thousand sequins I had given to each of them. I did

not, on this account, upbraid them. On the contrary, my stock being still six thousand sequins, I shared the half of it with them, telling them, 'My brothers, we must venture these three thousand sequins, and hide the rest in some secure place: that in case our voyage be not more successful than yours

We put to sea with a favourable wind.

was formerly, we may have wherewith to assist us, and to enable us to follow our ancient way of living.' I gave each of them a thousand sequins, and keeping as much for myself, I buried the other three thousand in a corner of my house. We purchased goods, and having embarked them on board a vessel, which we freighted between us, we put to sea with a favourable wind.

"After two months' sail, we arrived happily at port, where we landed and had a very good market for our goods. I especially sold mine so well, that I gained ten to one. With the produce we bought commodities of that country to carry back with us for sale.

"When we were ready to embark on our return, I met on the seashore a lady, exceedingly handsome, but poorly clad She walked up to me, kissed my hand, and besought me with great earnestness to marry her and take her along with me.

"She assured me that I should have all the reason in the world to be satisfied with her conduct, and begged me not to object to her on account of her poverty.

"And so at last I yielded, and ordered proper apparel to be made for her, and, after having married her, I took her on board, and we set sail. I found my wife possessed so many good qualities that my love for her increased every day In the meantime my two brothers, who had not managed their affairs as successfully as I had mine, envied my prosperity, and suffered their feelings to carry them so far, that they conspired against my life, and one night, when my wife and I were asleep, threw us both into the sea.

"My wife proved to be a fairy, and, by conse-

quence, a genie, so that she could not be drowned;
but for me, it is certain I must have perished without her help. I had scarcely fallen into the water,
when she took me up, and carried me to an island.

"When day appeared, she said to me, 'You see,
husband, that by saving your life, I have not re-

I met on the seashore a lady.

warded you ill for your kindness to me. You must
know that I am a fairy, and being upon the sea-
shore when you were going to embark, I felt a
strong desire to have you for my husband; I had a
mind to try your goodness, and presented myself
before you in disguise. You have dealt generously

by me, and I am glad of an opportunity of returning my acknowledgment. But I am incensed against
your brothers, and nothing will satisfy me but their
lives'

"I listened to this discourse with admiration and
thanked my wife the best way I could for the great
kindness she had done me. 'But, Madam,' said I,
'as for my brothers, I beg you to pardon them;
whatever cause of resentment they have given me,
I am not cruel enough to desire their death.'

"I pacified her by these words, and as soon as
I had concluded she transported me in a moment
from the island to the roof of my own house, and
then disappeared.

"I descended, opened the doors of my house, and
dug up the three thousand sequins I had formerly se-
creted I went afterwards to my shop, which I also
opened, and was complimented by the merchants,
my neighbours, upon my return. When I went back
to my house, I perceived there two black dogs,
which came up to me in a very submissive manner ·
I could not divine the meaning of this circumstance
until the fairy, my wife, appeared and said : 'Husband, be not surprised to see these dogs, they are
your brothers'

"I was troubled at this declaration, and asked
her by what power they were so transformed.

"'I did it,' said she, 'or at least authorised one
of my sisters to do it, who at the same time sunk

their ship. You have lost the goods you had on board, but I will compensate you another way As to your two brothers, I have condemned them to remain five years in that shape. Their perfidiousness too well deserves such a penance. At the end of that time, if you conduct them to my sister who placed the enchantment upon them she will remove it, and they will regain their natural forms.'

"The five years being now expired, I am travelling in quest of my wife's sister, and as I passed this way, I met this merchant and the good old man who led the hind, and sat down by them. This is my history, O Prince of Genies! do not you think it very extraordinary?"

"I own it is," replied the genie, "and on that account I remit the merchant the second half of the crime which he has committed against me," and with that the genie disappeared.

The merchant did not fail to make due acknowledgment to his deliverers. They rejoiced to see him out of danger, and, bidding him adieu, each of them proceeded on his way. The merchant returned to his wife and children, and passed the rest of his days with them in peace.

THE STORY OF THE FISHERMAN.

The fisherman.

THERE was once an aged fisherman, who was so poor that he could scarcely earn as much as would maintain himself, his wife, and three children. He went every day to fish betimes in the morning, and imposed it as a law upon himself not to cast his nets above four times a day.

He went out one morning before daybreak, and coming to the seaside cast in his nets. As he drew them towards the shore, he found them very heavy, and thought he had a good draught of fish, at which he rejoiced; but in a moment after, perceiving that instead of fish his nets contained nothing but the carcass of an ass, he was much vexed to have made such a sorry draught. He mended his nets, which were broken in several places, and threw them in a second time. When he would have withdrawn them he found a great deal of resistance, which made him think he had taken abundance of fish, but he found nothing except a basket full of gravel and slime, which grieved him extremely.

He threw away the basket, and, washing his nets from the slime, cast them the third time, but brought up nothing except stones, shells, and mud.

He examined the vessel on all sides.

No language can express his disappointment; he was almost distracted. However, as dawn began to appear he did not forget to say his prayers, like a good Mussulman, and he added to them this petition: "Lord, thou knowest that I cast my nets only four times a day; I have already drawn them three

times, without the least reward for my labour I am
only to cast them once more, I pray thee to render
the sea favourable to me."

The fisherman, having finished this prayer, cast
his nets the fourth time, and when he thought it
was proper drew them out, as formerly, with great
difficulty, but instead of fish, found nothing in them
but a vessel of yellow copper, which from its
weight seemed not to be empty; and he observed
that it was shut up and fastened with lead, having
the impression of a seal upon it. This turn of fortune rejoiced him. "I will sell it," said he, "to the
founder, and buy a measure of corn with the
money"

He examined the vessel on all sides, and shook
it, to try if its contents made any noise, but heard
nothing. This circumstance, and the fact that the
bottle was sealed with a leaden cover, made him
think that it contained something precious To try
this, he took a knife, and easily opened the bottle.

He turned the mouth downward, but nothing
came out, which surprised him extremely. He
placed it before him, but while he viewed it attentively there came out a very thick smoke, which
obliged him to retire two or three paces back

The smoke ascended to the clouds, and, extending itself along the sea and upon the shore, formed
a great mist, which we may well imagine filled the
fisherman with astonishment. When the smoke was

The smoke ascended to the clouds.

all out of the vessel, it re-united and became a solid body, of which was formed a genie twice as high as the greatest of giants. At the sight of a monster of such an unwieldy bulk, the fisherman would fain have fled, but was so frightened that he could not move

"Solomon," cried the genie immediately, "Solomon, great prophet, pardon, pardon; I will never more oppose your will, I will obey all your commands"

The fisherman, when he heard these words, recovered his courage· "Proud spirit," said he, "it is above eighteen hundred years since the prophet Solomon died, and we are now at the end of time. Tell me your history, and how you came to be shut up in this vessel."

"Presumptuous fellow," said the genie, turning to the fisherman with a fierce look. "Speak to me with more respect, I pray you, else will I kill you."

"Why would you kill me?" replied the fisherman. "Did I not just now set you at liberty, and have you already forgotten my services?"

"That will not save you," the genie answered, "I have only one favour to grant you, and that is the choice of what manner of death you would have me put you to."

"But wherein have I offended you?" demanded the fisherman.

"Hearken to my story," said the genie, "and

you will then understand the case. I am one of those rebellious spirits that opposed the will of Solomon, the great prophet. He therefore sent his servants to take me by force and bring me before him, and as I still persisted in refusing to submit to his authority he vowed to punish me. He therefore shut me up in this copper vessel; and that I might not break my prison he himself stamped the leaden cover with his great seal. He then gave the vessel to one of the genies who had submitted to him, with orders to throw me into the sea.

"During the first hundred years of my imprisonment, I swore that if anyone should deliver me before the expiration of that period, I would make him rich beyond belief. That century ran out, however, and during the second I made an oath that I would open all the treasures of the earth to anyone that might set me at liberty, but with no better success.

"In the third I promised to make my deliverer a powerful monarch, to be always near him in spirit, and to grant him every day three requests, no matter what they might be. But this century passed as the two former and I continued in my prison

"At last, being angry to find myself a prisoner so long, I swore that if, afterwards, anyone should deliver me, I would kill him without mercy, and grant him no other favour but to choose the manner of his death, and therefore, since thou hast delivered me to-day, I give thee that choice."

For some time the fisherman reasoned with the
genie, and endeavoured to dissuade him from his
purpose, but seeing that it was useless he determined
to resort to stratagem

"Since I must die then," said he to the genie,
"I submit to the will of heaven; but before I choose
the manner of my death, I conjure you by the great
name of the prophet Solomon to answer me truly
the question I am going to ask you."

The genie having promised to speak the truth,
the fisherman said to him "I wish to know if you
were really in this vessel, for I cannot believe it is
capable of holding one of your size."

"I swear to you that I was there, notwithstanding," replied the genie, "just as truly as you see me
here."

"Well," said the fisherman, "I cannot and will
not believe you, unless you go into the vessel again
to prove it to me"

Upon this the body of the genie began to dis-
solve, and changed itself into smoke, extending as
before upon the seashore, at last it began to collect itself and to re-enter the vessel, until no part
remained outside, when immediately a voice came
forth, which said to the fisherman

"Well now, incredulous fellow, do not you
believe me now?"

The fisherman, instead of answering the genie,
took the cover of lead, and, having speedily replaced

it on the vessel, cried out. "Now is it your turn to
beg my favour and to choose which way I shall put
you to death; but rather will I throw you into the
sea whence I took you. and I will build a house
upon the shore, where I will reside, and give notice
to all fishermen who come to throw in their nets
to beware of such a wicked genie, who has made a
vow to kill him that shall set you at liberty."

The genie struggled hard to set himself at
liberty, but finding this impossible, endeavoured to
persuade the fisherman to let him out of the bottle.
"What I said to you was only by way of jest,"
he said

"O genie," replied the fisherman, "but a moment ago you were one of the greatest of all genies,
and now are you one of the least. Your crafty discourse will signify nothing; to the sea you must
return, and there you shall stay until the day of
judgment. You rejected my prayers and I now
reject yours, and am resolved to throw you into
the sea "

"My good friend," replied the genie, "do not
be guilty of such cruelty. If you will let me out
I promise to do you no hurt, nay, far from that, I
will show you a way to become exceedingly rich."

The hope of delivering himself from poverty
prevailed with the fisherman, and after making the
genie take a great and solemn oath that he would
not harm him, he took the covering off the vessel.

In an instant the genie began to resume his form; no sooner had he done so than he kicked the bottle into the sea, laughed at the fisherman's alarmed face, and bade him follow him, bringing his nets with him

The fisherman took up his nets and followed him with some distrust They passed by the town, and came to the top of a mountain, from whence they descended into a vast plain, which brought them to a lake that lay between four hills.

When they reached the side of the lake the genie said to the fisherman. "Cast in your nets and catch fish"; the fisherman did so, never doubting that he would make a good catch, for he could see the waters were full of fish, and to his surprise they were of four colours, white, red, blue, and yellow.

He threw in his nets, and brought out one of each colour. Having never seen the like before, he could not but admire them, and, judging that he might get a considerable sum for them, he was very joyful

"Carry the fish to your sultan," said the genie, "and he will pay you well for them. You may come every day to fish in this lake, but I give you warning not to throw your nets above once a day, otherwise you will repent." Having spoken this, he struck his foot upon the ground, which opened, swallowed him up, and then closed again.

The fisherman, following the advice of the genie,

did not cast in his nets a second time, but returned
to the town and went immediately to the sultan's
palace to offer his fish.

The sultan was much surprised when he saw
them, and took them up and examined them closely
"Take them," said he to his vizier, "and carry them
to the cook, whom the Emperor of the Greeks has
sent me. I make no doubt they will prove as good
to the taste as to the sight."

The vizier carried them as he was directed, and,
delivering them to the cook, said "Here are four
fish which the sultan wishes you to dress."

He then returned to his master, who ordered
him to give the fisherman four hundred pieces of
gold, which he accordingly did.

The fisherman, who had never seen so much
money, could scarcely believe his good fortune, but
thought the whole must be a dream, until he found
it otherwise, by being able to provide necessaries
for his family with the produce of his fish.

Now as soon as the sultan's cook received the
fish, she prepared them and put them upon the fire
in a frying-pan, with oil, and when she thought them
fried enough on one side, she turned them upon the
other, but scarcely were they turned, when the wall
of the kitchen divided, and a young lady of wonderful beauty entered from the opening. She was clad
in flowered satin, after the Egyptian manner, with
pendants in her ears, a necklace of large pearls, and

bracelets of gold set with rubies, and carried a rod in her hand.

She moved towards the frying-pan, to the great amazement of the cook, and striking one of the fish with the end of the rod, said: "Fish, fish, are you faithful?" Then the four fish lifted up their heads and replied, "Yes, yes: if you reckon, we reckon; if you pay your debts, we pay ours."

As soon as they had finished these words, the lady overturned the frying-pan, and returned into the open part of the wall, which closed immediately, and became as it was before.

The cook was greatly frightened at what had happened, but as soon as she had sufficiently recovered she took up the fish that had fallen upon the hearth. But they were as black as coal

A young lady of wonderful beauty entered.

and not fit to be carried to the sultan. This troubled her greatly, and she fell to weeping.

"Alas!" said she, "what will become of me? If I tell the sultan what I have seen, I am sure he will not believe me, but will be enraged against me."

While she was thus bewailing herself, the

grand vizier entered, and asked her if the fish were ready

She told him all that had occurred, and the vizier sent word to the fisherman to bring four more such fish, as a misfortune had befallen the others, so that they were not fit to be carried to the sultan.

The fisherman, without saying anything of what the genie had told him, excused himself for that day on account of the long distance he had to traverse to reach the lake where he caught them, but promised to bring them without fail on the morrow

Accordingly he went away by night, and, coming to the lake, threw in his nets betimes next morning, took four fish like the former, and brought them to the vizier at the hour appointed

The minister took them and carried them to the kitchen, and shut himself up with the cook whilst she prepared them and put them on the fire, as she had done the four others the day previously. When they were fried on one side, and she had turned them upon the other, the kitchen wall again opened, and the same lady came in with the rod in her hand, struck one of the fish, spoke to it as before, and all four gave her the same answer. She then overturned the frying-pan with her rod and disappeared through the opening in the wall   The grand vizier, having witnessed all that had passed, said that it was too wonderful and extraordinary to be concealed from the sultan and that he would inform him therewith. This he did, and the sultan, being much surprised, sent immediately for the fisherman and said to him. "Friend, bring me four more such fish."

The fisherman, having undertaken to do so, went immediately to the lake, and at the first throwing in of his net he caught four fish and brought them immediately to the sultan, who ordered that four hundred pieces of gold should be given him.

As soon as the sultan had the fish he ordered them to be carried into his private room, with all that was necessary for frying them, and having shut himself up with the vizier, that minister prepared them and put them into the frying-pan, and when they were fried on the one side, turned them upon the other; then the wall opened, but instead of a young lady, there came out a black, in the habit of a slave, and of gigantic stature, with a great green staff in his hand. He addressed them in the same words the young lady had used and they answered as before, whereupon the black overturned the pan and the fish became black as coals. Having done this he disappeared through the opening in the wall

"After what I have seen," said the sultan, "I shall not be able to rest until I know what all this means."

He therefore sent for the fisherman and asked him where he had caught the fish he had brought to the palace.

"I fished for them in a lake situated between four hills," he answered, "beyond the mountains we see from hence."

The sultan then asked the vizier if he knew of such a lake. "No," replied the vizier, "I never so much as heard of it, although I have hunted beyond the mountains for over sixty years."

The sultan asked the fisherman how far the lake might be from the palace, and the fisherman having answered that it was not more than three hours' journey, the sultan ordered all his court to take horse, and commanded the fisherman to serve them as a guide.

They all ascended the mountain, and at the foot of it they saw, to their great surprise, a vast plain that nobody had observed till then, and at last they came to the lake, which they found to be situated between four hills as the fisherman had described. The water was so transparent, that they could see the fish swimming about and notice that they were like those the fisherman had brought to the palace.

The sultan then addressed his court and informed them that he was determined not to return to his palace until he had learned how the lake came to be in that place and why all the fish in it were of different colours.

Having spoken thus, he ordered his court to encamp; and immediately his pavilion and the tents of his household were planted upon the banks of the lake

When night came the sultan retired with his grand vizier and at once made known his plans to him.

"I intend," said he, "to withdraw myself from the camp; but I wish you to keep my absence a secret. Stay in my pavilion, and to-morrow morning, when the emirs and courtiers come to attend my levee, tell them that I am ill and wish to be alone; and the following days tell them the same thing, till I return. In the meantime I intend satisfying myself as to the cause of the strange occurrences we have witnessed."

In vain the grand vizier endeavoured to divert the sultan from this design, representing to him the dangers to which he might be exposed, but the sultan was resolved. He put on a suit of clothing suitable for walking, took his scimitar, and as soon as he found that all was quiet in the camp, went out alone and climbed to the top of one of the hills without much difficulty. He found the descent still more easy, and when he came to the plain, walked on until the sun arose, and then, at a considerable distance before him, he saw a vast building.

As he drew nearer he found it was a magnificent palace of black polished marble, covered with fine steel, as smooth as glass He advanced towards the gates, one of which was open, yet he thought it best to knock before entering. This he did, at first softly, but no one appearing, he knocked again and again, always louder and louder.

But no one came in answer to his summons and so he decided to enter "If there be no one in it," said he to himself, "I have nothing to fear; and if it be inhabited, I have wherewith to defend myself." So entering boldly, he cried "Is there no one here to receive a stranger, who comes for refreshment as he passes by?" The dead silence which followed his words increased his astonishment, and so, passing on his way, he came into a spacious court. There was no one to be seen, and he accordingly entered the grand halls, which were hung with silk tapestry The alcoves and sofas were covered with stuffs of Mecca, and the porches with the richest stuffs of India, mixed with gold and silver.

Next he came into a superb saloon, in the middle of which was a fountain, with a lion of massy gold at each angle water issued from the mouths of the four lions, and, as it fell, formed diamonds and pearls.

The palace was surrounded on three sides by gardens containing the most exquisite flowers, and to complete the beauty of the place an infinite number of birds filled the air with their harmonious notes.

The sultan walked from apartment to apartment, where he found everything rich and magnificent.

Suddenly he heard a voice raised in lamentable tones, and, listening with attention, distinguished these words:

"O fortune! thou who wouldst not suffer me longer to enjoy a happy lot, forbear to persecute me, and by a speedy death put an end to my sorrows.

The sultan drew near and saluted him.

Alas! is it possible that I am still alive, after so many torments as I have suffered?"

The sultan advanced towards the place whence the tones proceeded, and, coming to the door of a great hall, opened it, and saw a handsome young man of a melancholy countenance, richly habited, seated on a throne raised a little above the ground.

The sultan drew near and saluted him, whereupon the young man returned the salutation by an inclination of his head, and, without rising, at the same time he said.

"My lord, I am prevented by sad necessity from rising to receive you."

"As to the reason of your not rising, whatever your apology be, I heartily accept it," replied the sultan. "Being drawn hither by your complaints, I come to offer you my help Perhaps you will relate to me the history of your misfortunes. But inform me first, I pray you, the meaning of the lake near the palace, where the fish are of four colours Whose is this castle? How came you to be here? And why are you alone?"

Instead of answering these questions the young man began to weep bitterly, and upon the sultan praying him to relate the cause of his excessive grief, he said:

"Alas! my lord, how is it possible but I should grieve" At these words he lifted up his robe and showed the sultan that he was a man only from the head to the girdle, and that the other half of his body was black marble

"You must know, my lord," he continued, "that my father, named Mahmoud, was king of this country This is the kingdom of the Black Isles, which takes its name from the four small neighbouring mountains; for those mountains were formerly islands . the capital where the king, my father, resided, was situated on the spot now occupied by the lake you have seen.

"When my father died I succeeded him and immediately afterwards married my cousin. I was most tenderly attached to her and at first believed that my affection was returned. But one day, after we had been married five years, I overheard two of my wife's ladies conversing together when they believed me to be asleep.

"One of them said to the other· 'Is the queen not wrong that she does not love so amiable a prince? Every night she mixes the juice of a certain herb with his drink, and this makes him sleep so soundly that she is able to rise and leave him, and visit a black slave who instructs her in magic and all manner of wickedness that she will one day no doubt use to the harm of our good lord and master'

"You may guess, my lord, how much I was surprised at this conversation; but I feigned to awake without having heard a word. That night I supped with the queen, and when she presented me with a cup of liquid such as I was accustomed to drink, I went to a window which was open and threw out the drink so quickly that she had no knowledge of what I had done.

"Soon afterwards I lay down, and she, believing me to be asleep, said loud enough for me to hear 'Sleep on, and may you never wake again!'

"She then dressed herself and went out of the room. I robed myself in haste, took my scimitar, and followed her so quickly that I soon heard the sound of her feet before me. She passed through several gates, which opened upon her pronouncing some magical words, and the last she opened was that of the garden, which she entered. Passing through the garden she entered a little wood, where she was joined by an enormous black man. Listening intently, I heard them discuss the magical means by which my kingdom, castle, and subjects were to be ruined and overthrown, whilst I myself was to be made away with. I waited until the wicked pair passed by the spot where I had hidden myself, and then struck the black a terrific blow with my scimitar. The queen I spared, because she was my kinswoman I then retired speedily without having made myself known.

"The wound I had given the black was mortal; but by her enchantments she preserved him in an existence in which he could not be said to be either dead or alive. As for me, I returned to my bed well satisfied, and when I had rested some hours I arose as usual, dressed myself, and afterwards held my council When the queen next presented herself to me she was clad in deep mourning. I enquired of her the reason, and she informed me that she

had three distressing causes of affliction. 'I have just received news of the death of my mother,' said she; 'my father has been killed in battle, and my brother has fallen down a precipice.'

"I concluded from her making this excuse for her mourning that she had not suspected me of being the author of the black slave's misfortune, and offered her my sympathy and condolences in her grief.

"She asked leave to build for herself a palace of tears in which she could shut herself up and weep for those she had lost

"I consented to this, and when the building was complete she caused the black slave to be carried there, and used every art in her power to restore him to life But though, by her enchantments, she succeeded in preventing his actual death, she could not restore to him the power of speech, neither was he able to walk or support himself. Every day the queen paid him two long visits and worked her magic arts upon him, but without avail.

"One day my curiosity induced me to follow her to the Palace of Tears, and, having witnessed the tears she shed over the body of the wicked wretch upon whom only just punishment had fallen, I lost patience and discovered myself to her, telling her that such sorrow for a base and ungrateful slave was both dishonouring to her and myself

"The queen rose up in a fury and accused me

of being the cause of the misery which had overtaken the black magician

"'Yes,' I replied, 'it was I indeed who chastised
him, for I overheard him plotting the downfall of
my kingdom I ought to have treated you in like
manner, but spared you because you were my kinswoman. However, I have stayed my hand too long,
and I will now make an end of you both.'

"I raised my scimitar to strike, but she quickly
pronounced some words I did not understand, and
my arm became immovable; then, raising her voice,
she cried jeeringly 'By virtue of my enchantments
I command thee to become half marble and half
man.' Immediately, my lord, I became what you
see · a dead man among the living, and a living man
among the dead. After this cruel sorceress, unworthy
of the name of queen, had changed me thus and
brought me into this hall, by another enchantment
she destroyed my capital, which was very flourishing
and populous, changing it into the desert plain and
lonely lake which you have seen. The fishes in the
lake, of four different colours, are the four kinds of
inhabitants, of different religions, which the city contained. The white are the Mussulmen, the red the
Persians, who worship fire, the blue the Christians,
and the yellow the Jews. The enchantress herself
told me all this that she might add to my affliction.
But this is not all every day, taking advantage of
my helpless state, she comes and gives me, upon my

naked shoulders, a hundred lashes with a whip. When she has finished she throws over me a coarse gown of goat's hair, and over that this robe of brocade, not to honour, but to mock me."

The sultan was greatly moved by the recital of this affecting story, and, anxious to avenge the sufferings of the unfortunate prince, questioned him as to where he might find the wounded magician and the wicked queen.

The prince having informed him of the place in which the Palace of Tears was situated, added that every day at sunrise the queen visited her fellow conspirator and carried to him the potion which had hitherto prevented his dying, although he had never yet been able to regain the power of speech so that he might thank her for her attention to him.

By this time, the night being far advanced, the sultan retired to rest. He arose with the dawn and proceeded to the Palace of Tears. Entering, he soon perceived the bed upon which the black magician lay, and with one stroke from his scimitar deprived him of his wretched existence, dragged his body into the court of the castle, and threw it into a well.

After this he went and lay down in the bed, covering his face in such a manner that the queen could not detect the deception about to be practised upon her.

Before long she entered the apartment, and at

the sight of the prostrate figure she began to weep.
"Alas!" said she, "will you be always silent? Speak
one word to me at least, I conjure you"

"Unhappy woman," replied the sultan in hollow
tones, and counterfeiting the pronunciation of the
blacks, "art thou worthy that I should answer thee?
The cries and groans of thy husband, whom thou
treatest every day with such barbarity, prevent my
sleeping night or day. Had you disenchanted him,
I should long since have been cured, and have recovered the use of my speech"

"Well," said the enchantress, "what would you
have me do?"

"Make haste and set him at liberty, that I may
be no longer disturbed by his lamentations," replied
the sultan.

The enchantress immediately left the Palace of
Tears, and, taking a cup of water, she pronounced
some words over it which caused it to boil as if it
had been set over a fire. She afterwards proceeded
to the young king, her husband, and threw the water
upon him, saying "Resume your natural form."

Scarcely had she spoken the words than the
king found himself restored to his former condition

The enchantress then returned to the Palace of
Tears and, supposing she still spoke to the black,
informed the sultan of what she had done.

"What you have done is by no means sufficient," replied the sultan "The town and its in-

habitants still remain enchanted, and every night, at
midnight, the fish raise their heads out of the lake
and cry for vengeance against you and me. This is
the true cause of the delay of my cure. Go speedily
and restore things to their former state, and at
your return I will give you my hand and you shall
help me to arise."

The queen sprinkled the waters of the lake.

The queen went away at once, and when she
came to the brink of the lake she took a little water
in her hand and sprinkled the waters of the lake.
Immediately the whole city was restored to its former
magnificence, and Mohammedans, Christians, Persians,
and Jews, freemen or slaves, were as they were be-

fore, everyone having recovered his natural form
The sultan's numerous retinue found themselves en-
camped in the middle of a large, handsome, well-
peopled city.

As soon as the enchantress had effected this
wonderful change, she hastened to return to the
Palace of Tears. "I have done all that you required
of me," she cried, "I pray you then give me your
hand and rise"

"Come near," said the sultan, still counterfeiting
the pronunciation of the blacks, and as she did so
he suddenly rose, seized her by the arm, and with
one blow of his scimitar ended her wicked life.

This done he left her lying in the Palace of
Tears, and went to seek for the young King of the
Black Isles. When he found him the prince at
once embraced him with great affection and thanked
him with the greatest sincerity for all that he had
done for him

The sultan returned his embraces and said
to him

"You may henceforward dwell peaceably in
your capital, unless you will accompany me to mine,
which is but a few hours' journey distant."

"Potent monarch, to whom I owe so much,"
replied the young king, "it will take you a whole
year to return to your capital. I do indeed believe
that you came hither in the time you mention,
because my kingdom was enchanted; but since the

enchantment is taken off, things are changed. however, this shall not prevent my following you, were
it to the utmost corners of the earth. You are my
deliverer, and that I may give you proofs of my
acknowledging this during my whole life, I am
willing to accompany you, and to leave my kingdom
without regret."

The sultan was very much surprised to find he
was so far from his own dominions, but answered
the young king in the following words

"The trouble of returning to my own country
is sufficiently recompensed by acquiring you for a
son; for since you will do me the honour to accompany me, as I have no child, I look upon you
as such, and from this moment appoint you my heir
and successor."

Preparations were at once begun for the departure, the young king appointing one of his nearest of
kin to reign as monarch in his stead, and, after taking
affectionate leave of his subjects, he and the sultan
began their journey. They took with them a hundred
camels laden with inestimable riches from the king's
treasury, and were followed by fifty handsome
gentlemen on horseback, perfectly well mounted and
dressed. They had a pleasant journey, and when
they approached the capital the principal officers
came to receive the sultan and to assure him that
his long absence had occasioned no alteration in his
empire. The inhabitants also came out in great

crowds, received him with acclamations, and made public rejoicings for several days.

The sultan then acquainted his subjects with the news of his having adopted the King of the Black Isles as his son, and told them how he had been willing to leave a great kingdom to accompany and live with him.

As for the fisherman, as he was the first cause of the deliverance of the young prince, the sultan gave him a plentiful fortune, which made him and his family happy for the rest of their days

THE ENCHANTED HORSE.

The Hindoo.

THE first day of the year is observed throughout Persia as a solemn festival. Upon that day rejoicings are held and strangers are encouraged to come from the neighbouring states and most remote parts of the world, and are allowed to compete for large rewards, being invited to display to the sovereign the various inventions and contrivances they have brought with them.

Upon one of these festivals, after the most ingenious artists of the country had repaired to the Court at Sheeraz, had been entertained there by the king, and had been bountifully rewarded for their various productions, just as the assembly was about to break up, a Hindoo appeared at the foot of the throne. He had with him an artificial horse, richly caparisoned, and so naturally imitated that at first sight he was taken for a living animal.

The Hindoo prostrated himself before the

throne, and, pointing to the horse, said to the emperor, "Though I present myself the last before your Majesty, yet I can assure you that nothing shown to-day is so wonderful as this horse, on which I beg your Majesty would be pleased to cast your eyes."

"I see nothing more in the horse," replied the emperor, "than the natural resemblance the workman has given him, which the skill of another workman may possibly execute as well or better"

"Sir," replied the Hindoo, "it is not for his outward form and appearance that I recommend my horse to your Majesty's examination as wonderful, but the use to which I can apply him, and which, when I have communicated the secret to them, any other persons may make of him. Whenever I mount him, be it where it may, if I wish to transport myself through the air to the most distant part of the world, I can do it in a very short time. This, sir, is the wonder of my horse a wonder which nobody ever heard speak of, and which I offer to show your Majesty if you command me."

Notwithstanding the many prodigies of art the emperor had seen, he had never before beheld or heard of anything that came up to this. He told the Hindoo that unless he saw him perform what he had promised he could not bring himself to believe in the truth of it

The Hindoo instantly put his foot into the

stirrup, mounted the horse with admirable agility, and when he was seated in the saddle asked the emperor whither he would be pleased to command him to proceed.

About three leagues from Sheeraz there was a lofty mountain, discernible from the large square before the palace, where the emperor, his court, and a great concourse of people then were

"Do you see that mountain ?" said the emperor, pointing to it, "it is not a great distance from hence, but it is far enough to judge of the speed you can make in going and returning. But because the eye cannot follow you so far, as a proof that you have been there, I expect that you will bring me a branch of a palm-tree that grows at the bottom of the hill "

No sooner had the emperor spoken than the Hindoo turned a peg which was in the hollow of the horse's neck, just by the pommel of the saddle, and in an instant the horse rose off the ground and carried his rider into the air with the rapidity of lightning, to such a height that those who had the strongest sight could not discern him Within less than a quarter of an hour they saw him returning with the palm branch in his hand, but before he descended, he took two or three turns in the air and then alighted on the spot whence he had set off, without receiving the least shock from the horse to disorder him He dismounted, and, going up to

5

the throne, prostrated himself, and laid the branch of
the palm-tree at the feet of the emperor.

The emperor, who had viewed this extraordinary
sight with admiration as well as astonishment, conceived a great desire to have the horse, and thought
that he would have little difficulty in treating with
the Hindoo.

"Judging of the horse by his outward appearance,"
said he to the Hindoo, "I did not think him so
much worth my consideration As you have shown
me his merits, I am obliged to you for undeceiving
me; and to prove to you how much I esteem it, I
will purchase him of you, if he is to be sold."

"Sir," replied the Hindoo, "I never doubted
that your Majesty, who has the character of the most
liberal prince on earth, would set a just value on my
work as soon as I had shown you on what account
he was worthy your attention. I also foresaw that
you would not only admire and commend it, but
would desire to have it Though I know his intrinsic
value, and that my continuing master of him would
render my name immortal in the world, yet I am
not so fond of fame but I can resign him to gratify
your Majesty; however, in making this declaration,
I have another to add, without which I cannot resolve to part with him, and perhaps you may not
approve of it. I did not buy this horse, but obtained him from the inventor by giving him my only
daughter in marriage, and promising at the same

time never to sell him, but if I parted with him to exchange him for something that I should value beyond all else"

"I am willing,' said the emperor, "to give you whatever you may ask in exchange. My kingdom is large and contains great riches, I will give you the choice of what you like best."

This offer seemed royal and noble to the whole Court, but was much below what the Hindoo had in his mind

"I am infinitely obliged to your Majesty," he said, "and cannot sufficiently thank you for your generosity, yet I must beg of you not to be displeased if I have the presumption to tell you I cannot resign my horse unless I receive the hand of the princess, your daughter, as my wife."

The courtiers could not forbear laughing aloud at this extravagant demand of the Hindoo; but the Prince Firoze Shah, the eldest son of the emperor and heir to the crown, was most indignant

The emperor, however, was inclined to think he might sacrifice the Princess of Persia, so anxious was he to possess the horse.

Prince Firoze Shah, who saw his father hesitating what answer to make, began to fear lest he should comply with the Hindoo's demand; therefore, to anticipate him, he said—

"I hope your Majesty will forgive me for asking if it is possible your Majesty should hesitate about a

denial to so insolent a demand from such an insig-
nificant fellow? I beg you to consider what you owe
to yourself, to your own blood, and the high rank
of your ancestors"

"Son," replied the emperor, "I much approve
of your remonstrance, and am sensible of your zeal
for preserving the lustre of your birth; but you
do not consider sufficiently the excellence of this
horse; nor that the Hindoo, if I should refuse him,
may make the offer somewhere else, where this nice
point of honour may be waived I shall be in the
utmost despair if another prince should boast of
having exceeded me in generosity, and deprived me
of the glory of possessing what I esteem as the most
singular and wonderful thing in the world. I will
not say I cannot consent to grant him what he asked
Perhaps he has not well considered his exorbitant
demand and, putting my daughter, the princess, out
of the question, I may make another agreement with
him that will answer his purpose as well But before
I conclude the bargain with him, I should be glad
that you would examine the horse, try him yourself, and give me your opinion."

The Hindoo fancied, from what he had heard,
that the emperor was not entirely averse to his
alliance, and that the prince might become more
favourable to him; therefore, he expressed much joy,
ran before the prince to help him to mount, and
showed him how to guide and manage the horse

The prince mounted, however, without the Hindoo's assistance, and no sooner had he put his feet in both stirrups but, without staying for the owner's advice, he turned the peg he had seen him use, when instantly the horse darted into the air, quick as an arrow shot from a bow by the most adroit archer, and in a few moments the emperor, his father, and the numerous assembly lost sight of him. Neither horse nor prince were to be seen. The Hindoo, alarmed at what had happened, prostrated himself before the throne and said

"Your Majesty must have remarked the prince was so hasty that he would not permit me to give him the necessary instructions to govern my horse. Therefore the favour I ask of your Majesty is not to make me accountable for what accidents may befall him "

The emperor was much surprised and afflicted, and asked the Hindoo if there were no secret to bring him back, other than that by which he had been carried away.

"Sir," replied the Hindoo, "there is room to hope that the prince, when he finds himself at a loss, will perceive another peg, and as soon as he turns that, the horse will cease to rise, and descend to the ground, when he may turn him to what place he pleases by guiding him with the bridle "

Notwithstanding all these arguments of the Hindoo, which carried great appearance of probability, the Emperor of Persia was much alarmed at the evident danger of his son.

"I suppose," replied he, "it is very uncertain whether my son may perceive the other peg, and make a right use of it; may not the horse, instead of alighting on the ground, fall upon some rock, or tumble into the sea with him?"

"Sir," answered the Hindoo, "I can deliver your Majesty from this apprehension, by assuring you that the horse crosses seas without ever falling into them, and always carries his rider wherever he may wish to go. And your Majesty may assure yourself that if the prince does but find out the other peg I mentioned, the horse will carry him where he pleases It is not to be supposed that he will stop anywhere but where he can find assistance and make himself known."

"Be it as it may,' replied the Emperor of Persia, "as I cannot depend upon the assurance you give me, your head shall answer for my son's life if he does not return safely."

He then ordered his officers to secure the Hindoo, and keep him close prisoner, after which he retired to his palace in great affliction that the festival of the New Year should have proved so inauspicious.

In the meantime the prince was carried through the air with prodigious velocity, and in less than an hour's time had ascended so high that he could not distinguish anything on the earth, but mountains and plains seemed confounded together. It was then he began to think of returning, and conceived he might do this by turning the same peg the contrary way, and pulling the bridle at the same time. But when he found that the horse still rose with the same swift- ness, his alarm was great. He turned the peg several times, one way and the other, but all in vain. It was then he grew sensible of his fault in not having learnt the necessary pre- cautions to guide the horse before he mounted. How- ever, he examined the horse's head and neck with attention, and perceived behind the right ear another peg smaller than the other. He turned that peg and presently per- ceived that he descended in

The prince descended in the same manner.

the same manner as he had mounted, although not quite so swiftly.

Night had fallen over that part of the country in which the prince found himself when at length the horse stopped upon solid earth.

He was very faint from hunger, having eaten

nothing since the morning, when he came out of
the palace with his father to assist at the festival.

He found himself upon the terrace of a magnificent palace, and, groping about in the darkness, found a staircase which led down into an
apartment, the door of which was half open.

Few but Prince Firoze Shah would have ventured to descend those stairs, dark as it was, and
expose himself to dangers from unknown foes He
was quite unarmed, but, being of a courageous disposition, he opened the door wider, without making
any noise, went softly down the stairs, that he might
not awaken anybody, and, when he came to a landing
place on the staircase, found the door of a great
hall, that had a light in it, open

He stopped at the door and, listening, heard
no other noise than the snoring of some people
who were fast asleep He advanced a little into
the room, and by the light of a lamp saw that
those persons were black chamberlains, with naked
sabres laid by them, which was enough to inform
him that this was the guard-chamber of some
sultan or princess, which latter it proved to be.

In the next room to this the princess lay, as
appeared by the light streaming through a draped
doorway. Prince Firoze Shah advanced on tip-toe,
without waking the chamberlains He drew aside
the curtain, went in, and, without staying to observe
the magnificence of the chamber, gave his attention

to something of greater importance. He saw many
beds arranged upon the floor, and in these slept the
women attendants of the princess, whilst the princess
herself reposed upon a raised couch.

He crept softly towards the bed, without waking
either the princess or her women,
and beheld a beauty so extraordinary that he straightway fell
in love with her.

But having penetrated thus
far, the prince knew very well
that as soon as he was discovered he would be most certainly killed by the guards.
So he resolved to enlist the
sympathy of the princess. He
fell on his knees beside her and
gently twitched her sleeve. She
opened her eyes and, seeing a
handsome man on his knees,

The prince opened the door.

was greatly surprised, yet seemed to show no sign
of fear.

The prince bowed his head to the ground and,
rising, said:

"Beautiful Princess, by the most extraordinary
and wonderful adventure, you see at your feet a
suppliant prince, son of the Emperor of Persia, who
was yesterday in his Court, at the celebration of a
solemn festival, but is now in a strange country, in

danger of his life, if you have not the goodness and
generosity to afford him your assistance and protection.   These I implore with the confidence that you
will not refuse me, as one possessing so much beauty
and majesty must be incapable of entertaining any
but the most humane thoughts."

"Prince," she replied courteously, "you have
chanced upon no barbarous country   You are in the
kingdom of Bengal, and my father, who is the rajah,
will no doubt extend to you the protection you have
asked of me   But I would have you tell me," she
added, "by what miracle you have come hither from
the capital of Persia in so short a time, and by what
enchantment you have been able to penetrate so far
as to come to my apartment, and to have evaded the
vigilance of my guards ; yet as you must be sorely
in need of food and rest I will set aside my curiosity,
and give orders to my women to regale you and
show you an apartment, that you may rest yourself
after your fatigue and be the better able to satisfy
my curiosity."

The princess's women, who awoke at the first
words which the prince addressed to the princess,
were in the utmost surprise to see a man at the
princess's feet, as they could not conceive how he had
come thither without waking them or the chamberlains
They no sooner comprehended the princess's intentions
than they were ready to obey her commands.   They
each took a wax candle, of which there were great

numbers lighted up in the room, and after the prince
had respectfully taken leave, went before and conducted him into a handsome chamber, where, while
some were preparing the bed, others went into the
kitchen; and, notwithstanding the unreasonable hour,
they soon brought him a choice collation, and when
he had eaten as much as he chose, they removed

The prince fell on his knees beside her.

the trays and left him to taste the sweets of
repose.

In the meantime the Princess of Bengal was so
struck with the charms, wit, politeness, and other
good qualities which she had discovered in her short
interview with the prince, that she could not sleep:
but when her women came into her room again

questioned them as to the hospitality they had shown
him, and then proceeded to ask them more particularly what they thought of him

They assured her that they thought him as
handsome as he appeared amiable, that there was no
other prince in Bengal to be compared to him, and
that she would be happy indeed if her father were
to marry her to one so suited to her in every
way.

The next day the princess took more pains in
dressing and tiring herself at the glass than she had
ever done before, and also tried the patience of
her women beyond endurance, so anxious was she
to try on and take off again the various garments
she possessed, being dissatisfied with all of them.

At length she was habited in a garment of
the richest stuffs of the Indies, which is only made
for kings, princes, and princesses. She adorned
her head, arms, and waist with the finest and largest
diamonds she possessed, and after she had again
and again consulted her glass she asked her women,
one after another, if anything was wanting in her
attire

Being assured that she looked more lovely
than ever, she sent to know if the Prince of Persia
was awake, and, hearing that he was already up
and dressed, she went immediately to pay him a
visit.

"I would have received you in my own apartment," she informed him, "but as the chief of my guards has leave to come so far, though no further without my leave, I feared we might be interrupted; I therefore came to you, and beg you to gratify my curiosity as to the manner in which you came hither."

Prince Firoze Shah began the recital of his story with a description of the festival of the New Year, mentioning the various inventions which had been brought to court. Then he came to the enchanted horse, and, having described it minutely, said:

"You may well think, charming Princess, that the emperor, my father, who cares not what he gives for anything that is rare and curious, would be very desirous to purchase such a curiosity. He asked the Hindoo his price, and he replied that he would give the horse only in exchange for the princess, my sister, whom he wished to marry.

The Princess of Bengal.

"The crowd of courtiers who stood about the emperor, my father, laughed loudly at the extravagance of the demand; as for me, I was the more indignant as I saw my father was inclined to consent to the proposal, so anxious was he to possess the horse.

"The despicable Hindoo, thinking no doubt that he would bring me over to his opinion if once I understood the singular worth of his horse, invited me to make a trial of him.

"To please my father, I mounted the horse, and as soon as I was upon his back, put my hand on a peg, as I had seen the Hindoo do before, to make the horse mount into the air, and did not wait to receive instructions from the owner as to the way I should guide the animal The instant I touched the peg, the horse ascended as swift as an arrow, and I was presently at such a distance from the earth that I could not distinguish any object. From the swiftness of the motion I was for some time un-apprehensive of the danger to which I was exposed, when I grew sensible of it I endeavoured to turn the peg the contrary way. But the experiment did not answer, for still the horse rose, and carried me a greater distance from the earth.

"At last I perceived another peg, which I turned, and then I grew sensible that the horse descended towards the earth, and presently found myself so surrounded with darkness that it was impossible to guide the machine At length the horse stopped I alighted and, examining my whereabouts, found my-self upon the terrace of this palace. I descended the steps and, seeing a door open, entered, passed through the room in which the guards were asleep, and entered your chamber

"With what passed next you are not unacquainted. And now, I feel obliged in duty to thank you for your goodness and generosity. According to the law of nations I am already your slave, and cannot make you an offer of my person, there only remains my heart but alas! Princess, that is no longer my own, your charms have forced it from me, and I shall never ask for it again, but yield it up to you, and only beg for leave to declare you mistress of both my heart and inclination."

The princess blushed very prettily and replied that she had been very pleasurably entertained by the recital of the prince's wonderful adventures, declaring she could not forbear a shudder when she thought of the tremendous height he had been in the air, and avowing her delight that he had descended upon the terrace of her palace instead of in some other spot, as might very easily have happened.

"As to your being my slave," said she, "I should think myself offended if you seriously believed so Assure yourself you are here as much at liberty as in the midst of the Court of Persia."

At this moment one of the princess's women announced that a meal had been served, and the princess led him into a magnificent hall where a cloth was laid, the table being covered with a great variety of dainty and choice dishes. Having breakfasted, they rose, and the princess again conducted

the prince into a large and magnificent apartment,
where they sat down in a balcony overlooking the
gardens of the palace   Here they conversed very
pleasantly together, the prince describing his home
and country, and managing to draw very flattering
comparisons between the princess's beautiful palace
and those in his own country.

The princess, whilst assuring him that she had
no complaints to make of the palace allotted to
her, assured him that the one inhabited by her
father, the rajah, was far finer   She begged him,
since chance had brought him so near to her father's
capital, to pay him a visit there, in order that he
might receive the honours due to a prince of his
rank and merit.

The princess hoped that, by exciting in the
Prince of Persia a curiosity to see the capital of
Bengal, and to visit her father, the king, seeing him
so handsome, wise, and accomplished a prince, might
perhaps resolve to propose an alliance with him, by
offering her to him as a wife   And as she was in
no wise averse to the handsome young man herself,
this course would have pleased her vastly.   The
prince, however, did not return her an answer according to her expectations

"Princess," he replied, "the preference which
you give the Rajah of Bengal's palace to your own
is enough to induce me to believe it much exceeds
it : and as to the proposal of my going and paying

my respects to the king, your father, I should not only do myself a pleasure, but an honour But judge, Princess, yourself, would you advise me to present myself before so great a monarch like an adventurer, without attendants and a train suitable to my rank?"

"Prince," replied the princess, "let not that give you any pain, if you will but go, you shall want no money to have what train and attendants you please. I will furnish you; and we have traders here of all nations in great numbers, and you may make choice of as many as you please to form your household."

"I would most willingly accept this obliging offer," replied the prince, "for which, moreover, I cannot sufficiently show my gratitude, if I were not prevented by the thought of the uneasiness my father must feel on account of my absence. I should be unworthy of the tenderness he has always had for me if I did not return as soon as possible to calm his fears. Afterwards, Princess, if you will permit me, and think me worthy to aspire to the happiness of becoming your husband, I will obtain my father's leave to return, not as a stranger, but as a prince, to contract an alliance with your father by our marriage."

The Princess of Bengal was too reasonable, after what the Prince of Persia had said, to persist any longer in persuading him to pay a visit to the Rajah

6

of Bengal, or to ask anything of him contrary to his
duty and honour. But she begged him, at least, to
remain a few days longer in her palace, and so well
did she entertain him, that the days had extended
into months before the prince could manage to tear
himself away.

But at length, in declaring seriously that he
could stay no longer, he entreated her to accompany
him to his father's Court.

As the prince observed that the princess was
not averse to this suggestion, he continued to urge
it. "As for my father's consent, Princess," he said,
"I venture to assure you he will receive you with
pleasure; and as for the Rajah of Bengal, after all
the love and tender regard he has expressed for you
he must be the reverse of what you have described
him if he should not receive in a friendly manner
the embassy which my father will send to him for
his approbation of our marriage."

The princess returned no answer to this
address, but her silence, and eyes cast down, were
sufficient to inform him that she had no reluctance
to accompany him into Persia. Her one ob-
jection was the fear that the prince might not be
able to manage the enchanted horse; but on the
prince's declaration that he could guide it as
well as the Hindoo himself, she consented to accompany him.

The next morning, a little before daybreak,

The horse mounted into the air.

when all the attendants were asleep, the prince
and princess went out upon the terrace of the
palace. The prince turned the horse towards
Persia, and placed him where the princess could
easily get up behind him. which she had no sooner
done, and was well settled with her arms about
his waist for her better security, than he turned
the peg, when the horse mounted into the air
and, making his usual haste, under the guidance
of the prince, in two hours' time they reached
the capital of Persia

He would not alight at the great square from
whence he had set out, nor in the palace, but
directed his course towards a pleasure-house a little
distance from the capital. He led the princess into
a handsome apartment, where he told her that,
to do her all the honour that was due to her, he
would go and inform his father of their arrival,
and return to her immediately. He ordered the
servants to provide her with whatever she required, and took his leave.

He then ordered a horse to be saddled, and
set out for his father's palace. He was received
with loud acclamations of joy by the people,
and the emperor, his father, embraced him with
tears of love and tenderness in his eyes. He was
eagerly questioned as to his adventures, and enquiries were made as to the whereabouts of the
Hindoo's horse

He was only too anxious to relate all that had befallen him, and laid particular stress upon the kindness he had received at the hands of the Princess of Bengal, dwelt upon the love they bore to each other, and finally confessed that he had prevailed upon her to accompany him to Persia, riding with him upon the enchanted horse.

The prince set out for his father's palace.

"Sir," said the prince, "I feel assured you will not refuse your consent to our union, and the princess awaits your decision as anxiously as I do. She is now at the palace where your Majesty often goes for your pleasure."

"Son," replied the emperor, once more embracing him, "I not only consent to your marriage with the Princess of Bengal, but I will go and meet her myself, and will bring her to my palace and celebrate your nuptials this day."

The emperor than gave orders for his Court to make preparations for the princess's entry; the rejoicings were to be announced by the royal band of military music, and the Hindoo was to be taken from his prison and brought before him.

When this had been done the emperor said

"I secured your person that your life might answer for that of the prince, my son, whom, however, I have found again go, take your horse, and never let me see your face more."

The Hindoo had heard from those who brought him out of prison that Prince Firoze Shah had returned with a princess, and also was informed of the place where he had alighted and left her, and that the emperor was making preparations to go and bring her to his palace; and as soon as he left the emperor's presence he bethought himself of being revenged upon the emperor and the prince Without losing any time, he went directly to the palace, and, addressing himself to the keeper, told him he came from the Prince of Persia for the Princess of Bengal, that he was to conduct her, seated behind him upon the enchanted horse, through the air to the emperor, who waited in the great square of his palace, to gratify the whole Court and city with the wonderful sight.

The palace-keeper, who knew the Hindoo, and that the emperor had imprisoned him, gave the more credit to what he said, because he saw that he had been set at liberty. He presented him to the princess, who no sooner understood that he came from the prince than she consented to do as she believed the prince desired her.

The Hindoo, overjoyed at his success and the

ease with which he had accomplished his villainy,
mounted the horse, took the princess behind him,
turned the peg, and instantly the horse mounted
into the air

At the same time the emperor was on his
way to the palace, and the prince rode a little in
advance that he might prepare the princess to
receive his father. The Hindoo, thinking this an
excellent opportunity to brave them both, and revenge himself for the ill-treatment he had received,
appeared above their heads with his prize.

When the emperor saw what had happened,
he and all his courtiers assailed him with reproaches
and threats, but more they could not do; he was
beyond their power, and they returned to the
palace overwhelmed with rage and vexation.

But what was Prince Firoze Shah's grief at be-
holding the Hindoo hurrying away the princess,
whom he loved so passionately? He did not know
at first how he should act, but decided to at least attempt to recover the princess from the power of
the wicked Hindoo. He therefore continued his
way to the pleasure palace, where he had left the
princess

The palace-keeper, who knew by this time
that he had been too credulous, threw himself at
the prince's feet and entreated him to take his
life. "Rise," said the prince, "I do not impute
the loss of my princess to you, but to my own

want of precaution. But lose no time, fetch me
a dervish's habit, and take care you do not give
the least hint that it is for me."

Not far from the pleasure palace stood a convent
of dervishes, the superior of which was the palace-
keeper's friend, and from him he readily obtained
a complete dervish's habit and carried it to Prince
Firoze Shah. The prince dressed himself in it,
and, being thus completely disguised, took a box
of jewels which he had brought as a present for
the princess, and set out upon his travels, determined not to return until he had found his princess,
or to perish in the attempt.

But to return to the Hindoo. He managed
his enchanted horse so well, that he arrived early
next morning in a wood near the capital of the
kingdom of Cashmeer. Being hungry, and concluding
the princess was also, he alighted in the wood, and
left the princess reclining on a grassy spot, close to
a rivulet of clear water, whilst he went in search
of food.

The princess would willingly have attempted to
make her escape, but she was too much overcome
with fear, hunger, and fatigue to move from the spot.

When the Hindoo returned, she took eagerly
the food he gave her, for she wished to recover her
strength sufficiently to be able to outwit him, and
fortunately before long she heard the sound of horsemen advancing, and deeming that she could not very

well be in worse hands than those of the Hindoo,
she shrieked and cried for help

Fortunately the company of horsemen proved
to be the Sultan of Cashmeer and his attendants,
who, as they were returning from hunting, happily
for the Princess of Bengal, passed through that
part of the wood, and ran to her assistance.

The sultan addressed himself to the Hindoo,
demanded who he was, and wherefore he ill-treated
the lady. The Hindoo, with great impudence, replied that she was his wife, and no one had any
right to interfere between them.

The princess, who neither knew the rank nor
quality of the person who came so seasonably to her
relief, hastened to say.

"My lord, whoever you are, whom Heaven has
sent to my assistance, have compassion on a princess
in distress and give no credit to that impostor
Heaven forbid that I should be the wife of so vile
and despicable a Hindoo! A wicked magician, who
has forced me away from the Prince of Persia, to
whom I was going to be united, and has brought
me hither on the enchanted horse you behold
there."

The Princess of Bengal had no occasion to say
more to persuade the Sultan of Cashmeer that what
she told him was truth Her beauty, majestic air,
and tears spoke sufficiently for her. Justly enraged
at the insolence of the Hindoo, he ordered his

The sultan addressed himself to the Hindoo.

guards to surround him, and strike off his head. which sentence was immediately executed.

The princess, thus delivered from the persecutions of the Hindoo, fell into another no less afflicting. The sultan conducted her to his palace, where he lodged her in the most magnificent apartments, next his own, commanded a great number of women slaves to attend her, and ordered a suitable guard. He led her himself into the apartment he had assigned her, where, without giving her time to thank him for the great obligation she had received, he said to her

"As I am certain, princess, that you must want rest, I will take my leave of you till to-morrow, when you will be better able to relate to me the circumstances of this strange adventure."

He then left her.

The princess's joy was inexpressible at finding herself delivered from the Hindoo, and she flattered herself that the Sultan of Cashmeer would complete his generosity by sending her back to the Prince of Persia when she should have told him her story, but alas! she was deceived in her hopes, for the sultan had fallen in love with her and had resolved to marry her himself the next day. For that reason he ordered great rejoicings to be made, and the princess was awakened at daybreak by the beating of drums, the sounding of trumpets, and noise of other instruments expressive of joy.

When the sultan, who had given orders that he should be informed when the princess was ready to receive a visit, came to wait upon her, after he had enquired after her health, he acquainted her that all those rejoicings were to render their nuptials the more solemn, and at the same time desired her assent to the union.

This declaration put her into such agitation that she fainted away.

The women slaves who were present ran to her assistance, and when at length she began to recover from her swoon she resolved that, sooner than wed the sultan and be false to the prince, she would feign madness, thereby gaining a little time in which to make plans for her escape. So she began to utter the most extravagant expressions before the sultan, and even rose from her seat as if to attack him

He was greatly grieved, fearing that it was his sudden and unexpected proposal that had caused the attack. As his presence seemed to irritate her, he left her with her women, charging them to take the greatest care of her and never to leave her alone.

He sent many times during the day to enquire after her, but the reports he received were most unfavourable. The next day the princess was still no better, and the sultan sent for his Court physicians to ask if they could cure her

The princess, who feared if they examined her

too closely they would discover the trick she had
resorted to, pretended to fly into a fit of rage and
to be anxious to injure them, so that they were
all afraid to approach her. Some ordered her
potions, which she made no difficulty in taking,

The princess fainted away.

but which had no effect whatever in mitigating the
disease.

When the Sultan of Cashmeer saw that his Court
physicians could not cure her, he called in others,
but without effect. Then he sent messages to the
Courts of neighbouring sultans, begging that the most
famous physicians might be allowed to come and try
their skill upon the case of the princess.

Various physicians arrived from all parts and tried their skill, but none could boast of success, since it was a case that did not depend on medicine, but on the will of the princess herself.

During this time, Prince Firoze Shah, disguised in the habit of a dervish, travelled through many provinces and towns, not knowing which way to direct his course, or whether he might not be pursuing the very opposite road to which he ought, in order to hear tidings of the lost princess

He made diligent enquiry after her at every place he came to, till at last, passing through a city of Hindoostan, he heard the people talk much of a Princess of Bengal, who went mad the very day of her intended marriage with the Sultan of Cashmeer.

At the name of the Princess of Bengal, and supposing that there could exist no other Princess of Bengal than her upon whose account he had undertaken his travels, he hastened towards the kingdom of Cashmeer, and upon his arrival at the capital took up his lodging at a khan, where he heard the story of the princess and the fate of the Hindoo magician, and felt convinced that he had at length found the beloved object of his search The following day he provided himself with a physician's habit, and, having let his beard grow during his travels, he felt he could easily pass himself off as a physician. He went to the sultan's palace, where he presented

himself to the chief of the officers, and observed,
modestly, that perhaps it might be looked upon as
a rash undertaking to attempt to cure the princess
after so many had failed, but that he hoped some
specifics, from which he had
experienced success, might
effect the desired relief.

The chief of the officers
told him he was welcome,
that the sultan would receive
him with pleasure, and that
if he should have the good
fortune to restore the princess to her former health, he
might expect a considerable
reward from his master's
liberality.

The Sultan of Cashmeer,
who had begun to lose all
hope of the princess's recovery, when he heard of
the new physician's arrival
ordered him to be shown
into his presence. Then,
without wasting any time,

*The prince disguised
as a dervish.*

he told him the princess could not bear the sight
of any physician without falling into most violent
transports, which increased her malady; and took
him straightway to a little room from whence,

through a lattice, he might see her without being observed.

There Prince Firoze Shah beheld his lovely princess sitting with tears in her eyes, and singing an air in which she deplored her unhappy fate, which had deprived her, perhaps for ever, of the object she loved so tenderly.

The prince was much affected by the melancholy condition in which he found his dear princess, but he felt certain her malady was feigned for love of him, and so he told the sultan that he had discovered the nature of the complaint, and that it was not incurable, but added that it was absolutely necessary for him to speak with her alone.

The sultan ordered the princess's door to be opened, and Firoze Shah went in. As soon as the princess saw him (taking him by his habit to be a physician), she rose up in a rage, threatening and abusing him. He, however, went straight towards her, and said in a low voice, that no one else might hear, "Princess, I am not a physician, but the Prince of Persia, and am come to procure you your liberty."

The princess, who knew the sound of the voice, and the upper features of his face, notwithstanding he had let his beard grow so long, grew calm at once, and a secret joy and pleasure overspread her face. Firoze Shah told her as briefly as possible how despair had seized him when he

saw the Hindoo carry her away; the resolution he
afterwards had taken to leave everything to find her
out, and never to return home till he had regained
her, and by what good fortune, at last, after a long
and fatiguing journey, he had the satisfaction of
finding her in the palace of the Sultan of Cashmeer
He then desired the princess to inform him of all
that happened to her, from the time she was taken
away till that moment when he had the happiness
to converse with her, telling her that it was of the
greatest importance to know this, that he might take
the most proper measures to deliver her from the
tyranny of the Sultan of Cashmeer.

The princess, having informed him of all that
had happened, of her rescue from the Hindoo, and
of the sultan's subsequent intention of marrying her,
added that she had been able to think of no other
mode of escaping than to feign madness.

The prince then asked if she knew what had
become of the enchanted horse. The princess, however, knew nothing of its whereabouts, but was
quite sure the sultan had preserved it as a great
curiosity

As Firoze Shah never doubted but the sultan
had the horse, he told the princess that he intended making use of it to convey them both back
to Persia, and after they had consulted together
on the measures they should take, they agreed that
the princess should dress herself the next day, and

receive the sultan civilly, but without speaking
to him.

The sultan was overjoyed when the prince
stated to him the effect his first visit had had towards the cure of the princess. On the following
day, when the princess received him in such a
manner as persuaded him her cure was far advanced, he regarded him as the greatest physician
in the world; and, seeing her in this state, contented himself with telling her how rejoiced he was
at her being likely soon to recover her health.
He bade her follow the directions of so skilful a
physician, in order to complete what he had so
well begun, and then retired without waiting for
her answer.

The Prince of Persia asked the sultan how the
Princess of Bengal came into the dominions of
Cashmeer thus alone, since her own country was far
distant. This he said on purpose to introduce some
conversation about the enchanted horse, and to find
out what had become of it.

The sultan, who could not penetrate into the
prince's motive, concealed nothing from him, and
told him that he had ordered the enchanted horse
to be kept in his treasury as a great curiosity, though
he knew not the way to use it.

"Sir," replied the pretended physician, "the information which your Majesty has given your devoted
slave affords me a means of curing the princess. As

she was brought hither on this horse, and the horse is enchanted, she has contracted something of the enchantment, which can be dissipated only by a certain incense which I am acquainted with. If your Majesty would entertain yourself, your Court, and the people of your capital with the most surprising sight that ever was beheld, let the horse be brought into the great square before the palace, and leave the rest to me. I promise to show you and all that assembly, in a few moments' time, the Princess of Bengal completely restored in body and mind. But the better to effect what I propose, it will be requisite that the princess should be dressed as magnificently as possible, and adorned with the most valuable jewels your Majesty may possess."

The sultan having eagerly consented to all that was asked of him, preparations were made for the show to take place upon the following day.

In the morning, by the prince's orders, the horse was taken out of the treasury and placed in the great square before the palace.

A report having been spread through the town that there was something wonderful to be seen, crowds of people flocked from all parts, insomuch that the sultan's guards were placed around the horse to prevent disorder and to keep a space clear.

The Sultan of Cashmeer, surrounded by all his

nobles and ministers of state, was seated upon a
platform erected for the purpose. The Princess of
Bengal, attended by a number of ladies whom the
sultan had assigned her, went up to the enchanted
horse and mounted with the help of her women
When she was in the saddle, and had the bridle in
her hand, the pretended physician placed round the
horse, at a proper distance, many vessels full of
lighted charcoal, which he had ordered to be
brought, and, going round them with a solemn pace,
cast in a strong and sweet-smelling perfume; then,
with downcast eyes and his hands crossed upon
his breast, he paced three times round the horse,
pronouncing some mystical words. The moment the
pots of charcoal sent forth a dense cloud which
surrounded the princess, so that neither she nor
the horse could be seen, the prince jumped nimbly
up behind her, and reaching his hands to the peg,
turned it; and just as the horse rose in the air
he pronounced these words, which the sultan heard
distinctly.

"Sultan of Cashmeer, when you marry princesses
who implore your protection, learn first to obtain
their consent."

Thus the prince delivered the Princess of Bengal,
and carried her the same day to the capital of Persia,
where he alighted in the square before the palace
The emperor, his father, ordered every preparation
for the solemnization of the marriage to be made

immediately, and the ceremony was performed with due pomp and magnificence.

After the days appointed for the rejoicings were over, the Emperor of Persia's first care was to name and appoint an ambassador to go to the Rajah of Bengal with an account of what had happened, and to demand his approbation and ratification of the alliance contracted by this marriage; which the Rajah of Bengal took as an honour, and granted with great pleasure and satisfaction.

THE STORY OF ALADDIN
OR
THE WONDERFUL LAMP.

The lamp.

IN the capital of one of the large and rich provinces of the kingdom of China, there lived a tailor, named Mustapha, who was so poor that he could hardly, by his daily labour, maintain himself and his family, which consisted of a wife and son.

His son, who was called Aladdin, had been brought up in a very careless and idle manner, and by that means had contracted many bad habits. He was in the habit of going out early in the morning, and would stay out all day, playing in the streets and public places with idle children of his own age.

When he was old enough to learn a trade, his father, not being able to put him out to any other, took him into his own shop, and taught him how to use his needle but all his father's endeavours to keep him to his work were in vain, for no sooner was his back turned, than he was gone for that day. Mustapha chastised him, but Aladdin was incorrigible and his father, to his great grief, was forced to abandon him to his idleness, and was so much troubled at not being able to reclaim him, that it threw him into a fit of sickness, of which he died in a few months.

The mother, finding that her son would not follow his father's business, shut up the shop, sold off everything, and with the money she received, and what she could get by spinning cotton, endeavoured to maintain herself and her son.

Aladdin, who was now no longer restrained by the fear of a father, and who cared so little for his mother, gave himself entirely over to his idle companions. One day, as he was playing, according to custom, in the street with his vagabond associates, a stranger passing by stood to observe him.

This stranger was a magician who had recently arrived from Africa.

The African magician observing in Aladdin's countenance something absolutely necessary for the execution of the design he was engaged in, enquired artfully about his family, and when he had learned all he desired to know, went up to him, and, taking him aside from his comrades, said, "Child, was not your father called Mustapha the tailor?"

"Yes, sir," answered the boy; "but he has been dead a long time."

At these words, the African magician threw his arms about Aladdin's neck, and kissed him several times, with tears in his eyes.

Aladdin, who observed his tears, asked him what made him weep. "Alas! my son," cried the magician with a sigh, "how can I forbear? I am your uncle; your worthy father was my own brother. I have been many years abroad, and now I am come home with the hopes of seeing him, you tell me he is dead. I assure you it is a great grief to me to be deprived of the comfort I expected." Then he asked Aladdin, putting his hand into his purse, where his mother lived; and as soon as Aladdin had informed him, he gave him a handful of small money, saying, "Go, my son, to your mother, give my love to her, and tell her that I will visit her to-morrow, if I have time, that I may have the satisfaction of seeing where my good brother lived so long, and ended his days."

"Child, was or your father called Mustapha?"

As soon as the African magician had left his newly-adopted nephew, Aladdin ran to his mother,

overjoyed at the money his uncle had given him.
"Mother," said he, "have I an uncle?" "No,
child," replied his mother, "you have no uncle
by your father's side or mine." "I am just now
come," said Aladdin, "from a man who says he
is my uncle by my father's side, assuring me that
he is his brother. He cried and kissed me when
I told him my father was dead, and to show
you that what I tell you is truth," added he, pulling out the money, "see what he has given me;
he charged me to greet you and to tell you, if
he has any time to-morrow, he will come and pay
you a visit, that he may see the house my father
lived and died in" "Indeed, child," replied the
mother, "your father had a brother, but he has
been dead a long time, and I never heard of
another."

The mother and son talked no more then of
the African magician, but the next day Aladdin's
uncle found him playing in another part of the
town with other children, and, embracing him as
before, put two pieces of gold into his hand, and
said to him, "Carry this, child, to your mother,
tell her that I will come and see her to-night,
and bid her get us something for supper; but first
show me the house where you live."

This Aladdin did, and afterwards carried the
two pieces of gold to his mother, and when he
had told her of his uncle's intention, she went

out and bought provisions. She spent the whole day in preparing the supper, and at night, when it was ready, said to her son, "Perhaps your uncle knows not how to find our house, go and bring him if you meet with him."

Just then somebody knocked at the door, which Aladdin immediately opened, and the magician came in loaded with wine and all sorts of fruits. These he put into Aladdin's hands, saluted his mother, and desired her to show him the place where his brother Mustapha used to sit on the sofa; and when she had so done he fell down and kissed it several times, crying out with tears in his eyes, "My poor brother! how unhappy am I, not to have come soon enough to give you one last embrace!"

The magician then sat down and began to enter into discourse with Aladdin's mother "My good sister," said he, "do not be surprised at your never having seen me all the time you have been married to my brother Mustapha of happy memory. I have been forty years absent from this country, which is my native place, as well as my late brother's, and during that time have travelled into the Indies, Persia, Arabia, Syria and Egypt, have resided in the finest towns of those countries, and afterwards crossed over into Africa, where I made a longer stay. At last, as it is natural for a man, I was desirous to see my native country again

and to embrace my dear brother. I will not tell
you the length of time it took me, and what I
have endured to come hither; but nothing ever
mortified and afflicted me so much as hearing of
my brother's death, for whom I always had a
brotherly love and friendship I observed his
features in the face of my nephew, your son, and
distinguished him among a number of children with
whom he was at play. It is a comfort for me to
find, as it were, my brother in a son who has
his most remarkable features."

The African magician then addressed himself
to Aladdin and asked him his name. "I am called
Aladdin," said he.

"Well, Aladdin," replied the magician, "what
business do you follow?"

At this question the youth hung down his
head, and was not a little abashed when his mother
answered, "Aladdin is an idle fellow, his father
strove all he could to teach him his trade, but
could not succeed, and since his death, notwithstanding all I can say to him, he does nothing
but idle away his time in the streets as you saw
·him. For my part, I am resolved one of these
days to turn him out of doors, and let him provide
for himself."

After these words Aladdin's mother burst into
tears; and the magician said, "This is not well,
nephew; you must think of helping yourself and

getting your livelihood. Perhaps you did not like your father's trade and would prefer another. If you have no mind to learn any handicraft, I will take a shop for you. Consult your inclination, and tell me freely what you think of my proposal; you shall always find me ready to keep my word."

This plan greatly flattered Aladdin He told the magician he had a greater inclination to that business than to any other, and that he should be much obliged to him for his kindness. "Since this is agreeable to you," said the magician, "I will take you with me to-morrow, clothe you as hand-somely as the best merchant in the city, and after-wards we will think of opening a shop as I mentioned."

The widow, who never till then could believe that the magician was her husband's brother, no longer doubted after his promise of kindness to her son. She thanked him for his good intentions, and as the night was pretty far advanced the magician took his leave and retired.

He came again next day, as he had promised, and took Aladdin with him to a merchant, and after choosing a suit for himself, he bade Aladdin choose one he preferred. Aladdin, charmed with the liberality of his new uncle, made choice of one, and the magician immediately paid for it

When Aladdin found himself so handsomely

dressed, he returned his uncle thanks; who, on his part, promised never to forsake him.

He then showed him round the city and took him to the largest and finest mosques, and to the khans or inns where the merchants and travellers lodged; and afterwards to the sultan's palace, where he had free access; and at last brought him to his own khan, where, meeting with some merchants he had become acquainted with since his arrival, he gave them a treat to bring them and his pretended nephew acquainted.

Aladdin stood watching at the door.

The entertainment lasted till night, when Aladdin would have taken leave of his uncle to go home; the magician would not let him go by himself, but conducted him to his mother, who, as soon as she saw him so well dressed, was transported with joy. "Generous relation!" said she, "I know not how to thank you for your liberality! I know that my son is not deserving of your favours. I thank you with all my soul, and wish you may live long enough to witness my son's gratitude, which he cannot better show than by regulating his conduct by your good advice."

"Aladdin," replied the magician, "is a good boy, and I believe we shall do very well. I am sorry I cannot perform to-morrow what I promised, because, as it is Friday, the shops will be shut I will, however, call on him to-morrow and take him to walk in the gardens where people of the best fashion generally resort." The African magician took leave of the mother and the son and retired.

Aladdin rose early the next morning, dressed himself and stood watching at the door. As soon as he perceived his uncle coming, he told his mother, took leave of her, and ran to meet him.

The magician caressed Aladdin and said "Come, my dear child, and I will show you fine things." He then led him out at one of the gates of the city, to some magnificent houses, or rather palaces, with beautiful gardens into which anybody might enter. After pursuing their walk through the gardens, the African magician led Aladdin a long way into the country, till they nearly reached the mountains.

Aladdin, who had never been so far before, began to find himself much tired, and said to the magician, "Where are we going, Uncle? We have left the gardens a great way behind us, and I see nothing but mountains; if we go much

further, I do not know whether I shall be able
to reach the town again." "Never fear, nephew,"
said the false uncle, "I will show you another
garden which surpasses all we have yet seen."
Aladdin was soon persuaded, and the magician, to

Beautiful gardens into which anybody might enter.

make the way seem shorter and less fatiguing,
told him a great many stories.

At last they arrived between two mountains
divided by a narrow valley, which was the place
where the magician intended to execute the design
that had brought him from Africa to China. "We
will go no further now," said he to Aladdin; "I
will show you here some extraordinary things,

8

which, when you have seen, you will thank me
for: but while I strike a light gather up all the
loose dry sticks you can see, to kindle a fire
with "

Aladdin found so many dried sticks, that before
the magician had lighted a match, he had collected
a great heap. The magician presently set them
on fire, and when they were in a blaze, threw
in some incense, which raised a cloud of smoke
This he dispersed on each side, by pronouncing
several magical words which Aladdin did not
understand.

At the same time the earth, trembling, opened,
and uncovered a stone, laid horizontally, with a
brass ring fixed into the middle. Aladdin was so
frightened at what he saw, that he would have
run away; but the magician caught hold of him,
abused him, and gave him such a box on the ear
that he knocked him down. Aladdin got up trembling, and with tears in his eyes said, "What
have I done, Uncle, to be treated in this severe
manner?" "I have my reasons," answered the
magician: "I am your uncle, I supply the place
of your father, and you ought to make no reply.
But child," added he, softening, "do not be afraid;
for I shall not ask anything of you, but that you
obey me punctually. You see what I have done
by virtue of my incense and the words I pronounced. Know then that under this stone there

is hidden a treasure, destined to be yours, and which will make you richer than the greatest monarch in the world."

"Well, Uncle," said Aladdin, "what is to be

done? Command me; I am ready to obey." "I am overjoyed, child," said the magician, embracing him, "take hold of the ring, and lift that stone." "Indeed, Uncle," replied Aladdin, "I am not strong enough; you must help me." "You have no occasion for my assistance," answered the magician; "if I help you, we shall be able to do nothing; take hold of the ring, pronounce the names of your

Aladdin raised the stone with ease.

father and grandfather, then lift it up, and you will find it will come easily." Aladdin did as the magician bade him, raised the stone with ease, and laid it on one side.

When the stone was pulled up, there appeared a cavity of about three or four feet deep, with a little door, and steps to go down lower. "Observe, my son," said the African magician, "what I direct. Descend into the cave, and when you are at the bottom of those steps you will find a door open, which will lead you into a spacious vault, divided into three great halls, in each of which you will see four large brass cisterns placed on each side, full of gold and silver; but take care you do not meddle with them. Above all things, have a care that you do not touch the walls, so much as with your clothes; for if you do so you will die instantly At the end of the third hall you will find a door which opens into a garden planted with fine trees laden with fruit; walk directly across the garden by a path which will lead you to five steps that will bring you upon a terrace, where you will see a niche before you, and in that niche a lighted lamp. Take the lamp down, and extinguish it: when you have thrown away the wick and poured out the liquor, put it in your vestband and bring it to me. If you should wish for any of the fruit of the garden, you may gather as much as you please."

After these words, the magician drew a ring off his finger, and put it on one of Aladdin's, telling him that it was a preservative against all evil, while he should observe what he had prescribed to him After this instruction he said, "Go down boldly, child, and we shall both be rich all our lives."

Aladdin jumped into the cave, descended the steps, and found the three halls just as the African

magician had described. He went through them
with all the precaution the fear of death could
inspire, crossed the garden without stopping, took
down the lamp from the niche, threw out the
wick and the liquor, and, as the magician desired,
put it in his vestband. On his return he stopped
in the garden to observe the fruit, of which he
had only caught a glimpse before. All the trees
were loaded with extraordinary fruit, of different
colours. The white were pearls; the clear and
transparent, diamonds; the deep red, rubies, the
green, emeralds; the blue, turquoises; the purple,
amethysts, and those that were of yellow cast,
sapphires. Aladdin would have preferred figs and
grapes, or any other fruit, but although he took
them for coloured glass of little value, yet he was
so pleased with the variety of the colours that he
resolved to gather some of every sort.

Aladdin having loaded himself with riches he
knew not the value of, returned through the three
halls and soon arrived at the mouth of the cave,
where the African magician expected him with the
utmost impatience. As soon as Aladdin saw him
he cried out, "Pray, Uncle, lend me your hand,
to help me out" "Give me the lamp first," replied
the magician, "it will be troublesome to you."
"Indeed, Uncle," answered Aladdin, "I cannot now,
but I will as soon as I am up"

The African magician insisted that he would

have the lamp before he would help him up; and Aladdin, who had encumbered himself so much with his fruit that he could not well get at it, refused to give it to him till he was out of the cave. The magician, provoked at this obstinate refusal, flew into a passion, threw a little of his incense into the fire, and no sooner pronounced two magical words, than the stone which had closed the mouth of the cave moved into its place, with the earth over it in the same manner as it lay at the arrival of the magician and Aladdin.

This action plainly showed him to be not Aladdin's uncle but a true magician. From his youth he had applied himself to the study of magic, and after forty years' experience in enchantments and reading of magic books, he had found that there was in the world a wonderful lamp, the possession of which would render him more powerful than any monarch But though he had a certain knowledge of the place where the lamp was, he was not permitted to take it himself, but must receive it from the hands of another person. For this reason he had addressed himself to Aladdin, whom he looked upon as a young lad whose life was of no consequence, and fit to serve his purpose, resolving, as soon as he should get the lamp into his hands, to sacrifice him to his avarice and wickedness so that no witness would remain of the transaction.

When he saw that all his hopes were frus-
trated for ever, he started the same day on his
return to Africa, but avoided the town lest some
persons who had observed him walk out with the
boy, on seeing him come back without him, should
entertain any suspicions and stop him.

According to all appearances, there was no
prospect of Aladdin being any more heard of. But
the magician, when he had contrived his death,
forgot the ring he had put upon his finger, which
preserved him, though he knew not its virtue.

The surprise of Aladdin, who had never
suspected this treachery from his pretended uncle,
is more easily to be imagined than expressed
When he found himself buried alive, he cried and
called out to his uncle, to tell him he was ready
to give him the lamp, but in vain, since his cries
could not be heard. He descended the steps with
a design to get into the garden, but the door,
which was opened before by enchantment, was
now shut by the same means. He then redoubled
his cries and tears, sat down on the steps, without
any hope of ever seeing light again, and in a
melancholy certainty of passing from the present
darkness into that of speedy death

Aladdin remained in this state two days, without eating or drinking, and on the third looked
upon death as inevitable. He clasped his hands
with an entire resignation to the will of God, and

in this action of joining his hands, he rubbed the ring which the magician had put on his finger, and immediately a genie of enormous size rose out of the earth, his head reaching the roof of the vault, and said to him—"What would you have? I am ready to obey you as your slave, and the slave of all who may possess the ring on your finger: I and the other slaves of that ring."

At another time Aladdin would have been frightened at the sight of so extraordinary a figure, but the danger he was in made him answer without hesitation, "Whoever you are, deliver me from this place, if you are able." He had no sooner spoken these words than he found himself on the very spot where the magician had caused the earth to open. He was much surprised not to find the earth open, and could not comprehend how he had got so soon out of the cave. There was nothing to be seen but the place where the fire had been. Rejoicing to find himself once more in the world, he made the best of his way home. When he got within his mother's door, the joy to see her, and his weakness for want of food, made him faint, and he remained for a long time as dead. As soon as he recovered, the first words he spoke were: "Pray, Mother, give me something to eat, for I have not put a morsel of anything into my mouth these three days." His mother brought him what she had, and set it be-

A genie of enormous size rose out of the earth.

fore him. "My son," said she, "be not too eager,
for it is dangerous; eat but little at a time."

Aladdin took his mother's advice, and ate and
drank moderately. He then related to her all that
had happened to him. Aladdin's mother listened
with much patience, but when
she heard of the perfidy of the
African magician she could not
help breaking out into abuse,
calling him perfidious traitor,
barbarian, assassin, deceiver, magician, and an enemy and des-
troyer of mankind. She said a
great deal more against the
magician's treachery, but finding
that whilst she talked Aladdin,
who had not slept for three days
and nights, began to doze, she
left him to his repose and retired.

Aladdin was faint.

Aladdin, who had not closed his eyes while
he was in the subterranean abode, slept very
soundly till late the next morning, when the first
thing he said to his mother was, that he wanted
something to eat, and that she could not do him
a greater kindness than to give him his breakfast.
"Alas! child," said she, "I have not a bit of
bread to give you, you ate up all the provisions
I had in the house yesterday; but have a little

patience, and it shall not be long before I will bring you some; I have a little cotton, which I have spun I will go and sell it, buy bread and something for our dinner." "Mother," replied Aladdin, "keep your cotton for another time, and give me the lamp I brought home with me yesterday, I will go and sell it, and the money I shall get for it will serve both for breakfast and dinner, and perhaps supper too."

Aladdin's mother took the lamp and said to her son, "Here it is, but it is very dirty; if it were a little cleaner I believe it would bring something more." She took some fine sand and water to clean it, but had no sooner begun to rub it than in an instant a genie of gigantic size appeared before her, and said to her in a voice like thunder, "What would you have? I am ready to obey you as your slave, and the slave of all those who have that lamp in their hands; I and the other slaves of the lamp."

Aladdin's mother, terrified at the sight of the genie, fainted; when Aladdin, who had seen such a phantom in the cavern, snatched the lamp out of her hand, and said to the genie boldly, "I am hungry, bring me something to eat." The genie disappeared immediately, and in an instant returned with a large silver tray, holding twelve covered dishes of the same metal, which contained the most delicious meats, six large white bread cakes on

two plates, two flagons of wine, and two silver
cups. All these he placed upon a carpet, and disappeared: this was done before Aladdin's mother
recovered from her swoon.

Aladdin fetched some water and sprinkled it
on her face, and it was not long before she came
to herself.

"Mother," said Aladdin, "get up and come
and eat; here is what will put you in heart, and
at the same time satisfy my extreme hunger; do
not let such delicious meat get cold."

His mother was much surprised to see the
food. "Child," said she, "to whom are we obliged
for this great plenty and liberality? Has the sultan
been made acquainted with our poverty, and had
compassion on us?" "It is no matter, Mother,"
said Aladdin, "let us sit down and eat, for you
have almost as much need of a good breakfast
as myself; when we have done I will tell you"

The mother and son sat long at breakfast, so
delicious was the food, and when Aladdin's mother
had taken away and set by what was left, she
went and sat down by her son on the sofa, saying, "I expect now that you should satisfy my
impatience, and tell me exactly what passed between
the genie and you while I was in a swoon",
which he readily complied with.

She was in as great amazement at what her
son told her as at the appearance of the genie,

and said to him, "But son, what have we to do
with genies? I never heard that any of my acquaintance had ever seen one. How came that vile
genie to address himself to me, and not to you,
to whom he had appeared before in the cave?"
"Mother," answered Aladdin, "the genie you saw
is not the one who appeared to me, though he
resembles him in size, no, they had quite different
persons and habits; they belong to different masters.
If you remember, he that I first saw called himself the slave of the ring on my finger, and this
you saw, called himself the slave of the lamp you
had in your hand, but I believe you did not hear
him, for I think you fainted as soon as he began to
speak."

"What!" cried the mother, "was your lamp
then the occasion of that genie's addressing himself to me rather than to you? Ah! my son,
take it out of my sight, and put it where you
please. I will never touch it. I had rather you
would sell it than run the hazard of being frightened
to death again by touching it, and if you would
take my advice, you would part also with the
ring, and not have anything to do with genies."

"With your leave, Mother," replied Aladdin,
"I shall now take care how I sell a lamp which
may be so serviceable both to you and me.
Have not you been an eye-witness of what it has
procured us? It shall continue to furnish us with

money; who, after the first time, durst not offer
him less, for fear of losing so good a bargain.
When he had sold the last dish, he had recourse
to the tray, which weighed ten times as much as
the dishes, and would have carried it to his old
purchaser, but that it was too large and cumber-
some, therefore he was obliged to bring him home
with him to his mother's, where, after the Jew
had examined the weight of the tray, he laid down
ten pieces of gold, with which Aladdin was very
well satisfied.

They lived on these ten pieces in a frugal
manner, and Aladdin, though used to an idle life,
had left off playing with lads of his own age ever
since his adventure with the African magician.
He spent his time in walking about and conversing
with decent people, with whom he gradually got
acquainted. Sometimes he would stop at the principal merchants' shops, where people of distinction
met, and listen to their discourse, by which he
gained some little knowledge of the world.

When all the money was spent, Aladdin had
recourse again to the lamp. He took it in his
hand, looked for the part where his mother had
rubbed it with the sand, rubbed it also, when the
genie immediately appeared, and said, "What would
you have? I am ready to obey you as your slave,
and the slave of all those who have that lamp
in their hands; I and the other slaves of the

lamp." "I am hungry," said Aladdin, "bring me something to eat." The genie disappeared, and presently returned with a tray, on which were the same number of covered dishes as before, set it down, and vanished.

Aladdin's mother, knowing what her son was going to do, went out about some business, on purpose to avoid being in the way when the genie came, and when she returned was almost as much surprised as before at the prodigious effect of the lamp. However, she sat down with her son, and when they had eaten as much as they liked, she set enough by to last them two or three days.

As soon as Aladdin found out their provisions were expended, he took one of the dishes and went to look for his Jew again, on his way he passed a goldsmith's shop, the owner of which had the character of a very fair and honest man The goldsmith perceiving him, called to him, and said, "My lad, I have often observed you go by loaded as you are at present, and talk with a certain Jew, and then come back again empty-handed I imagine that you carry something which you sell to him, but perhaps you do not know that he is the greatest rogue even among the Jews, and is so well known, that nobody of prudence will have anything to do with him. If you will show me what you now carry, and it is to be sold, I will give you the full worth of it, or I will direct you to other merchants who will not cheat you.'

The hopes of getting more money for his plate induced Aladdin to pull it from under his vest, and show it to the goldsmith, who at first sight saw that it was made of the finest silver, and asked

"*What a villain!*" *cried the goldsmith.*

him if he had sold such as that to the Jew, when Aladdin told him that he had sold him twelve such, for a piece of gold each. "What a villain!" cried the goldsmith; "but," added he, "my son, what is past cannot be recalled. By advising you the value of this plate, which is of the finest silver

we use in our shops, I will let you see how much
the Jew has cheated you."

The goldsmith took a pair of scales, weighed
the dish, and after he had mentioned how much
an ounce of fine silver cost, assured him that his
plate would fetch by weight sixty pieces of gold,
which he offered to pay him immediately.

Aladdin thanked him for his fair dealing, so
greatly to his advantage, took the gold, and never
after went to any other person, but sold him all
his dishes and the tray, and had as much for them
as the weight came to.

Though Aladdin and his mother had an inex-
haustible treasure in their lamp, and might have
had whatever they wished for, yet they lived with
the same frugality as before, except that Aladdin
dressed better; as for his mother, she only wore
such clothes as she earned by spinning cotton.
After their manner of living, it may easily be supposed that the money for which Aladdin had sold
the dishes and tray was sufficient to maintain them
some time.

During this interval, Aladdin frequented the
shops of the principal merchants, where they sold
cloth of gold and silver, linens, silks, stuffs and
jewellery, and, oftentimes joining in their conversation, acquired a knowledge of the world and re-
spectable demeanour. By his acquaintance among
the jewellers he came to know that the fruits which

he had gathered when he took the lamp were, instead of coloured glass, stones of inestimable value, but he had the prudence not to mention this to anyone, not even to his mother.

One day as Aladdin was walking about the town he happened to meet the Princess Buddir al Buddoor, the sultan's daughter, attended by a great crowd of ladies and slaves. When she came within three or four paces of Aladdin the wind lifted a corner of her veil, which gave him an opportunity of seeing her charming face. The princess was noted throughout the world for her beauty, and it is not surprising therefore that Aladdin, who had never before seen such a blaze of charms, was dazzled, enchanted. It was some time after the princess had passed by before Aladdin recovered from his astonishment and went home He could not, however, forget the princess, and his mother, perceiving that he was more thoughtful and melancholy than usual, asked what had happened to make him so, or if he were ill. He returned her no answer, but sat carelessly down on the sofa, and remained silent, musing on the image of the charming Buddir al Buddoor. His mother served the supper, but Aladdin could eat little

After supper she asked him again why he was so melancholy Aladdin answered by telling her all that had occurred that day, and ended by say-

ing, "I love the princess more than I can express; and as my passion increases every moment,
I cannot live without the amiable Buddir al Buddoor, and am resolved to ask her in marriage of
the sultan her father."

Aladdin's mother listened with surprise to what
her son had told her; but when he talked of asking
the princess in marriage, she thought he must have
taken leave of his senses.

"Indeed, son," replied the mother seriously,
"I cannot help telling you that you have forgotten
yourself, and if you would put this resolution of
yours into execution, I do not see whom you can
prevail upon to venture to make the proposal for
you." "You, yourself," replied he immediately. "I
go to the sultan!" answered the mother, amazed
and surprised, "I shall be cautious how I engage
in such an errand. Why, who are you, son," continued she, "that you can have the assurance to
think of your sultan's daughter? Have you forgotten that your father was one of the poorest
tailors in the capital, and that I am of no better
extraction, and do not you know that sultans never
marry their daughters but to princes, sons of sover-
eigns like themselves?"

"Mother," answered Aladdin, "I have already
told you that I foresaw all that you have said, or
can say; and tell you again that neither your discourse nor your remonstrances shall make me

change my mind. I have told you that you must ask the princess in marriage for me: it is a favour I desire of you, and I beg of you not to refuse, unless you would see me in my grave."

"But reflect, my son," replied the mother, "nobody ever asks a favour of the sultan without taking a present, and what present have you that is fit to offer? Consider well, you aspire to an object which it is impossible for you to obtain."

Aladdin heard very calmly all that his mother could say to dissuade him from his design, and replied, "I own, Mother, it is great rashness in me to presume to carry my pretensions so far, but I love the princess, or rather, I adore her, and shall always persevere in my design of marrying her You say it is not customary to go to the sultan without a present, and that I have nothing worthy of his acceptance. As to the necessity of a present, I agree with you, and own that I never thought of it; but as to what you say, that I have nothing fit to offer, do not you think, Mother, that what I brought home with me from the cave may be an acceptable present? I mean what you and I both took for coloured glass; but now I am un-deceived, and can tell you that they are jewels of great value and fit for the greatest monarchs. I know the worth of them by frequenting the shops, and you may take my word that all the precious stones which I have seen in the shops are not to

be compared to those we have, either for size or
beauty. You have a large porcelain dish fit to
hold them; fetch it, and let us see how they will
look when we have arranged them according to
their different colours."

Aladdin's mother brought the china dish, when
he took the jewels out of the two bags in which he
had kept them, and placed them in order according
to his fancy. But the brightness and lustre they
emitted in the daytime, and the variety of the
colours, dazzled the eyes of both mother and son.

After they had admired the beauty of the
jewels some time, Aladdin said to his mother, "Now
you cannot excuse yourself from going to the
sultan under pretext of not having a present to
make him, since here is one which will gain you
a favourable reception."

"My son," said the good woman, "I cannot
conceive that our present will have its desired
effect, or that the sultan will look upon me with
a favourable eye, I am sure that if I attempt to
deliver your strange message I shall have no power
to open my mouth, therefore I shall not only
lose my labour, but the present, which you say
is so valuable; and shall return home again in
confusion to tell you that your hopes are frus-
trated, but," added she, "I will exert my best
endeavours to please you."

She used many arguments to endeavour to

make him change his mind, but the charms of the
princess had made too great an impression on
Aladdin's heart for him to be dissuaded from his
design. He persisted in importuning his mother to
execute his resolution, and she, as much out of
tenderness as for fear he should be guilty of greater
extravagance, complied with his request.

As it was now late, and the time for admis-
sion to the palace was passed, it was put off till
the next day. "Child," said the mother to Aladdin, "if the sultan should receive me as favourably
as I wish for your sake, should even hear my
proposal with calmness, and after this scarcely-to-
be-expected reception should think of asking me
where lie your riches and your estate (for he will
sooner enquire after these than your person), if, I
say, he should ask me these questions, what answer
would you have me return him?"

"Let us not be uneasy, Mother," replied Aladdin, "about what may never happen. First, let us
see how the sultan receives, and what answer he
gives, you If it should so fall out that he desires
to be informed of what you mention, I have thought
of an answer, and am confident that the lamp which
has supported us so long will not fail me in time
of need."   ·

The tailor's widow could not say anything
against what her son then proposed, but reflected
that the lamp might be capable of doing greater

wonders than just providing them with food. This
consideration satisfied her, and at the same time
removed all the difficulties which might have prevented her from undertaking the service she had
promised her son with the sultan; Aladdin, who
penetrated into his mother's thoughts, said to her,
"Above all things, Mother, be sure to keep secret
our possession of the lamp, for thereon depends
the success we have to expect;" and after this
caution Aladdin and his mother parted to go to
rest. But violent love, and the great prospect of
so immense a fortune, had so much possessed the
son's thoughts that he could not repose himself so
well as he could have wished He rose before
daybreak, awakened his mother, pressing her to go
to the sultan's palace and to get admittance, if
possible, before the grand vizier, the other viziers
and the great officers of state went in to take
their seats in the divan, where the sultan always
assisted in person.

Aladdin's mother took the china dish, in which
they had put the jewels the day before, wrapped
in two napkins, one finer than the other, which
was tied at the four corners for more easy carriage,
and set forwards for the sultan's palace. When
she came to the gates, the grand vizier, the other
viziers and most distinguished lords of the Court
were just gone in, but, notwithstanding the crowd
of people, she got into the divan, a spacious hall,

the entrance into which was very magnificent. She placed herself just before the sultan, grand vizier and the great lords who sat in council on his right and left hand. Several causes were called, according to their order, pleaded and adjudged,

The sultan.

until the time the divan generally broke up, when the sultan rising, returned to his apartment, attended by the grand vizier; the other viziers and ministers of state then retired, as also did all those whose business had called them thither: some pleased with gaining their causes, others dissatisfied at the sentences pronounced against them, and some in expectation of theirs being heard the next sitting.

Aladdin's mother, seeing the sultan retire, and all the people depart, judged rightly that he would not sit again that day, and resolved to go home. When Aladdin saw her return with the present designed for the sultan, he knew not what to think of her success, and in his fear lest she should bring him some ill news, had not courage to ask her any questions; but she told him speedily what had happened, and how she had found no opportunity of speaking to the sultan, promising, however, to go again the following day.

Though his passion was very violent, Aladdin was forced to be satisfied with this delay, and to fortify himself with patience. He had at least the satisfaction to find that his mother had got over the greatest difficulty, which was to procure access to the sultan, and hoped that the example of those she saw speak to him would embolden her to acquit herself better of her commission when a favourable opportunity might offer to speak to him

The next morning she repaired to the sultan's palace with the present, as early as the day before, and when she came there she found the gates of the divan shut, and understood that the council sat but every other day, therefore she must come again the next. She went six times afterwards on the days appointed, placed herself always directly before the sultan, but with as little success as on the first morning, and might have perhaps gone a thousand times to as little purpose, if luckily the sultan himself had not taken particular notice of her; for only those who came with petitions approached the sultan, when each pleaded their cause in its turn, and Aladdin's mother was not one of them.

On the sixth day, however, after the divan was broken up, when the sultan returned to his own apartment, he said to his grand vizier, "I have for some time observed a certain woman, who attends constantly every day that I give

audience, with something wrapped up in a napkin.
Do you know what she wants?"

As the grand vizier did not know, the sultan
said: "If she comes to our next audience, do not
fail to call her, that I may hear what she has
to say."

By this time the widow was so much used to
go to audience, and stand before the sultan, that
she did not think it any trouble, if she could but
satisfy her son that she neglected nothing that lay
in her power to please him. The next audience
day she went to the divan, placed herself in front
of the sultan as usual, and before the grand vizier
had made his report of business, the sultan perceived her, and, compassionating her for having
waited so long, said to the vizier, "Before you
enter upon any business, remember the woman I
spoke to you about; bid her come near, and let
us hear and despatch her business first."

So Aladdin's mother was called, and when
she had prostrated herself before the sultan, he
said: "Good woman, I have observed you to stand
a long time, from the beginning to the rising of
the divan; what business brings you here?"

Aladdin's mother prostrated herself again and
answered. "I beg of your Majesty, if you should
think my demand the least offensive, to assure me
first of your pardon and forgiveness" "Well,"
replied the sultan, "I will forgive you, be it what

it may, and no hurt shall come to you, speak boldly."

When Aladdin's mother had taken all these precautions, for fear of the sultan's anger, she told him faithfully how Aladdin had seen the Princess Buddir al Buddoor, the violent love that fatal sight had inspired him with, the declaration he had made to her of it when he came home, and what representations she had made to dissuade him from a passion "no less disrespectful," said she, "to your Majesty, as sultan, than to the princess your daughter. But," continued she, "my son, instead of taking my advice, was so obstinate as to persevere, and to threaten me with some desperate act if I refused to come and ask the princess in marriage of your Majesty; and it was not without the greatest reluctance that I was led to accede to his request, for which I beg your Majesty once more to pardon not only me, but also Aladdin my son, for entertaining so rash a project."

The sultan hearkened to this discourse with mildness, and without showing the least anger, but before he gave her any answer, asked her what she had brought tied up in a napkin. She took the china dish, which she had set down at the foot of the throne, untied it, and presented it to the sultan.

The sultan's amazement and surprise were inexpressible; he received the present from the hand of Aladdin's mother, crying out in a transport of joy, "How rich, how beautiful!" After he had admired and handled all the jewels, one after another, he turned to his grand vizier and, showing him the dish, said, "Behold, admire, wonder, and confess that your eyes never beheld jewels so rich and beautiful before." The vizier was charmed. "Well," continued the sultan, "what say you to such a present? Is it not worthy of the princess, my daughter? And ought I not to bestow her on one who values her at so great price?"

These words put the grand vizier into extreme agitation. The sultan had some time before signified to him his intention of bestowing the princess on a son of his; therefore he was afraid, and not without grounds, that the sultan, dazzled by so rich and extraordinary a present, might change his mind. He went to him, and, whispering him in the ear, said, "I cannot but own that the present is worthy of the princess, but I beg of your Majesty to grant me three months before you come to a final resolution. I hope, before that time, my son, on whom you have had the goodness to look with a favourable eye, will be able to make a nobler present than Aladdin, who is an entire stranger to your Majesty."

The sultan, though he was fully persuaded that it was not possible for the vizier to provide his son with so considerable a present, yet, as he had given him hopes, hearkened to him, and granted his request Turning, therefore, to the old widow, he said to her, "Good woman, go home, and tell your son that I agree to the proposal you have made me, but I cannot marry the princess my daughter yet, as the preparations for the wedding could not be finished for three months; but at the expiration of that time come again."

Aladdin's mother returned home much more gratified than she had expected, since she had met with a favourable answer, instead of the refusal and confusion she had dreaded. When she had told her son of the result of her mission, Aladdin thought himself the most happy of all men, and thanked his mother for the pains she had taken in the affair.

When two of the three months were past, his mother went one evening to buy some oil, and on coming into the city found a general rejoicing. The shops, instead of being shut up, were open, drest with foliage, silks and carpeting Aladdin's mother asked the oil-merchant what was the meaning of all this preparation of public festivity. "Whence came you, good woman," said he, "that you do not know the grand vizier's son is to marry the Princess Buddir al Buddoor, the sultan's daughter, to-night? These officers whom you see are to assist at the cavalcade to the palace, where the ceremony is to be solemnized"

This was news enough for Aladdin's mother
She ran, till she was quite out of breath, home to
her son, who little suspected any such event.
"Child," cried she, "you are undone! You depend
upon the sultan's fine promises, but they will come
to nothing. This night the grand vizier's son is
to marry the Princess Buddir al Buddoor." She
then related how she had heard it, so that from
all circumstances he had no reason to doubt the
truth of what she said.

Aladdin was thunderstruck. Any other man
would have sunk under the shock; but a sudden
hope of disappointing his rival soon roused his
spirits, and he bethought himself of the lamp,
which had on every emergency been so useful to
him, and without venting his rage in empty words
against the sultan, the vizier, or his son, he only
said, "Perhaps, Mother, the vizier's son may not
be so happy as he promises himself while I go
into my chamber a moment, do you get supper
ready." She accordingly went about it, but guessed
that her son was going to make use of the lamp
to prevent the marriage.

When Aladdin was in his chamber, he took
the lamp, rubbed it in the same place as before,
when immediately the genie appeared, and said to
him, "What would you have? I am ready to obey
you as your slave, and the slave of all those who
have that lamp in their possession; I and the other

slaves of the lamp" "Hear me," said Aladdin;
"you have hitherto brought me whatever I wanted
as to provisions, but now I have business of the
greatest importance for you to execute. I have
demanded the Princess Buddir al Buddoor in
marriage of the sultan her father; he promised her
to me, only requiring three months' delay, but
instead of keeping that promise, he has this night
married her to the grand vizier's son. What I
ask of you is that as soon as they are married
you bring them both hither" "Master," replied
the genie, "I will obey you"

Aladdin having then left his chamber, supped
with his mother, with the same tranquillity of mind
as usual, and after supper talked of the princess's
marriage as of an affair wherein he had not the
least concern; he then retired to his own chamber
again to await the execution of his orders to the
genie.

In the meantime everything was prepared with
the greatest magnificence in the sultan's palace to
celebrate the princess's nuptials, and the evening
was spent with all the usual ceremonies and great
rejoicings till midnight.

When the company had dispersed, the genie
proceeded to execute Aladdin's commands, and
transported the bride and bridegroom in an instant
into Aladdin's chamber. No sooner had he set
them down than Aladdin ordered the genie to

take the young man and shut him up, and come again the next morning before daybreak. The genie did as he was told, and after he had breathed upon him, which prevented his stirring, left him

Passionate as was Aladdin's love for the princess, he did not talk much to her when they were alone, but only said, with a respectful air, "Fear nothing, adorable princess, you are here in safety. If I have been forced to this extremity it is only to prevent an unjust rival possessing you, contrary to the sultan's promise in favour of myself."

The princess, who knew nothing of these particulars, gave very little attention to what Aladdin could say. The fright and amazement of so surprising and unexpected an adventure had alarmed her so much that he could not get one word from her.

Aladdin had no occasion the next morning to rub the lamp to call the genie, who appeared at the hour appointed, and said to him, "I am here, Master, what are your commands?" "Go," said Aladdin, "fetch the vizier's son out of the place where you left him, and take him and the princess to the sultan's palace from whence you brought them."

The genie presently returned with the vizier's son, and in an instant transported them into the palace from whence they had been brought. All this time, however, the genie was never visible either to the princess or the grand vizier's son. Neither did they hear anything of the discourse between Aladdin and him; they only perceived their transportation from one place to another, which we may well imagine was enough to alarm them.

The following day the princess was very melancholy, and the sultan, finding that he could not get a word from her, went immediately to the sultaness and told her in what state he had found the princess, and asked her to see whether she received her in the same manner. This she did, but for some time the princess refused to speak to her mother, but at last was induced to tell all that had befallen her.

The sultaness heard all the princess told her very patiently, but would not believe it, more especially as the vizier's son, when questioned, denied the story, being afraid he would be thought mad if he acknowledged it However, when night fell, and the festivities, which had again been kept up all day, were over, Aladdin once more sent the genie of the lamp to bring the newly-married couple to his house, and they passed the night in the same discomfort and terror as the previous one.

The vizier's son now began to think he had to pay somewhat dearly for being the sultan's son-in-law, and to wish the marriage might be annulled and he left in peace once more.

The princess when questioned told the sultan her father all that happened, and he, convinced that she spoke the truth, bade the grand vizier question his son.

This he did, and the poor bridegroom was only too anxious to own that he had misled them the previous day. With tears in his eyes he begged his father to express to the sultan how deeply he felt the honour that had been conferred upon him by the alliance, but to beg that he might be allowed to retire from the palace, alleging it was not just that the princess should be a moment longer exposed to so terrible a persecution.

The grand vizier found no great difficulty in obtaining what he asked, as the sultan had determined already; orders were given to put a stop to all rejoicings in the palace and town, and expresses despatched to all parts of his dominions to countermand them, and in a short time all rejoicings ceased.

This sudden and unexpected change gave rise both in the city and kingdom to various speculations and enquiries; but no other account could be given of it, except that both the vizier and his son went out of the palace very much dejected. Nobody but Aladdin knew the secret. He rejoiced within himself at the happy success procured by his

lamp. Neither the sultan nor the grand vizier, who
had forgotten Aladdin and his request, had the
least thought that he had any concern in the
enchantment which caused the dissolution of the
marriage.

Aladdin waited till the three months were
completed which the sultan had appointed before
the marriage between the Princess Buddir al Buddoor
and himself was to take place, and the next day
sent his mother to the palace to remind the sultan
of his promise.

Aladdin's mother went to the palace, and stood
in the same place as before in the hall of audience.
The sultan no sooner cast his eyes upon her than
he knew her again, remembered her business, and
how long he had put her off; therefore when the
grand vizier was beginning to make his report the
sultan interrupted him, and said, "Vizier, I see the
good woman who made me the present of jewels
some months ago, forbear your report till I have
heard what she has to say."

Aladdin's mother came to the foot of the throne,
prostrated herself as usual, and when she rose the
sultan asked her what she would have. "Sir,'
said she, "I come to represent to your Majesty,
in the name of my son Aladdin, that the three
months at the end of which you ordered me to
come again are expired, and to beg you to remember your promise."

The sultan, when he had fixed a time to answer the request of this good woman, little thought
of hearing any more of a marriage which he imagined
must be very disagreeable to the princess, when he
considered the meanness and poverty of the widow's
dress and appearance, but this summons for him to
fulfil his promise was somewhat embarrassing, he
declined giving an answer till he had consulted
his vizier.

The grand vizier advised him to the best of
his ability. "In my opinion, sire," said he, "there
is a way for your Majesty to avoid the match
without giving Aladdin any cause of complaint,
which is, to set so high a price upon the princess
that, however rich he may be, he cannot comply
with it."

The sultan, approving of the grand vizier's advice, turned to the tailor's widow, and said to her,
"Good woman, it is true sultans ought to abide
by their word, and I am ready to keep mine, by
making your son happy in marriage with the princess my daughter. But as I cannot marry her
without some further valuable considerations from
your son, you may tell him I will fulfil my promise
as soon as he shall send me forty trays of massive
gold, full of the same sort of jewels you have
already made me a present of, and carried by the
like number of black slaves, who shall be led by
as many young and handsome white slaves, all

dressed magnificently On these conditions I am ready to bestow the princess my daughter upon him, therefore, good woman, go and tell him so, and I will wait till you bring me his answer."

Aladdin's mother prostrated herself a second time before the sultan's throne, and retired. When she came home she said to her son, "Indeed, child, I would not have you think any further of your marriage with the princess. The sultan received me very kindly, and I believe he was well inclined to you. After I had represented to his Majesty that the three months were expired, and begged of him to remember his promise, I observed that he whispered with his grand vizier before he gave me his answer." She then gave her son an exact account of what the sultan had said to her, and the conditions on which he consented to the match. Afterwards she said to him, "The sultan expects your answer immediately; but," continued she, laughing, "I believe he may wait long enough "

"Not so long, Mother, as you imagine," replied Aladdin; "the sultan is mistaken if he thinks by this exorbitant demand to prevent my entertaining thoughts of the princess. I expected greater difficulties, and that he would have set a higher price upon her incomparable charms."

As soon as his mother was gone out to market, Aladdin took the lamp and, rubbing it, the genie

appeared, and offered his service as usual. "The
sultan," said Aladdin to him, "gives me the
princess his daughter in marriage, but demands
first forty large trays of massive gold, full of the
fruits of the garden from whence I took this lamp,
and these he expects to have carried by as many
black slaves, each preceded by a young handsome
white slave, richly clothed. Go and fetch me this
present as soon as possible, that I may send it to
him before the divan breaks up." The genie told
him his command should be immediately obeyed,
and disappeared.

In a little time afterwards the genie returned
with forty black slaves, each having on his head
a heavy tray of pure gold, full of pearls, diamonds,
rubies, emeralds and every sort of precious stones,
all larger and more beautiful than those presented
to the sultan. Each tray was covered with silver
tissue, embroidered with flowers of gold; these,
together with the white slaves, quite filled the
house, which was but a small one, the little court
before it and a small garden behind. When his
mother returned from market Aladdin said. "Lose
no time, Mother, but go at once to the palace
with this present as the dowry demanded for the
princess"

Without waiting to listen to his mother's ex-
clamations of surprise, he opened the street door,
and made the slaves walk out, bearing the precious

burdens with them. His mother followed, and he, Aladdin, shut the door.

When this splendid cavalcade reached the palace and was shown into the sultan's presence, Aladdin's mother advanced and said "Sir, my son is sensible this present is much below the Princess Buddir al Buddoor's worth, but hopes nevertheless that your Majesty will accept it."

The moment the sultan cast his eyes on the forty trays, full of the most precious, brilliant and beautiful jewels he had ever seen, and the four-score slaves, who appeared by the elegance of their persons and the richness and magnificence of their dress like so many princes, he was so struck that he could not recover from his admiration. Instead of answering Aladdin's mother, he addressed himself to the grand vizier.

"Well, Vizier," said he aloud, "who do you think it can be that has sent me so extraordinary a present? Do you think him worthy of the Princess Buddir al Buddoor, my daughter?"

The vizier, notwithstanding his envy and grief to see a stranger preferred to be the sultan's son-in-law before his son, durst not display his sentiments. It was too visible that Aladdin's present was more than sufficient to merit his being received into royal alliance; therefore, consulting his master's feelings, he returned his answer · "I am so far from having any thoughts that the

person who has made your Majesty so noble a
present is unworthy of the honour you would do
him, that I should say he deserved much more,
if I were not persuaded that the greatest treasure
in the world ought not to be put in competition
with the princess, your Majesty's daughter." This
speech was applauded by all the lords who were
then in council

The sultan made no longer hesitation, but
turned to Aladdin's mother and said, "My good
lady, go and tell your son that I wait with open
arms to embrace him, and the more haste he makes
to come and receive the princess my daughter from
my hands, the greater pleasure he will do me."

As soon as the tailor's widow had retired,
overjoyed as a woman in her condition must have
been, to see her son raised beyond all expectations
to such exalted fortune, the sultan put an end to
the audience, and, rising from his throne, ordered that
the princess's chamberlains should come and carry
the trays into their mistress's apartment, whither
he went himself to examine them with her at his
leisure. The fourscore slaves were conducted into
the palace, and the sultan, telling the princess of
their magnificent appearance, ordered them to be
brought before her apartment, that she might see
through the lattices he had not exaggerated in his
account of them.

Aladdin's mother hastened home and gave the

sultan's message to her son. He immediately retired to his chamber, and taking up the lamp,
summoned the genie and ordered him to convey
him to the bath, and afterwards to provide him
with a magnificent suit of apparel, and a charger
that should surpass in beauty the best in the sultan's
stables. "I also require," said he, "twenty slaves,
richly clothed, to walk by my side, and twenty more
to go before me. My mother must also be provided
with suitable raiment and with six women slaves to
attend her, and I require ten purses containing ten
thousand pieces of gold."

Almost as soon as Aladdin had given these orders
they were carried out, and Aladdin, sumptuously
attired and riding a magnificent charger, set out for
the palace. When he arrived there he found everything prepared for his reception and was led at
once into the sultan's presence.

The sultan was astonished to see him more
richly and magnificently habited than ever he had
been himself, and was struck by his good mien,
fine shape, and a certain air of unexpected dignity,
very different from the meanness of his mother's
late appearance.

But, notwithstanding, his amazement and surprise did not hinder him from rising off his throne
and descending two or three steps quick enough to
prevent Aladdin's throwing himself at his feet. He
embraced him with all the demonstrations of joy

at his arrival. He then led him into a spacious hall where a delicious collation was laid out. The sultan and Aladdin ate by themselves, and conversed together very pleasantly. At the conclusion of the meal the sultan was so confirmed in the high opinion he had formed of his future son-in-law that he suggested the marriage should be solemnized that very day.

"Sir," said Aladdin, "though great is my impatience to avail myself of your Majesty's goodness, yet I beg you to give me leave to defer it till I have built a palace fit to receive the princess, therefore I petition you to grant me a convenient spot of ground near your palace, that I may the more frequently pay my respects."

"Sir," said the sultan, "take what ground you think proper; there is space enough on every quarter round my palace, but consider I cannot see you too soon united to my daughter."

After these words he embraced Aladdin, who took his leave with as much politeness as if he had been bred up and always lived at Court.

No sooner had he reached home than he again summoned the genie. "Genie," said he, "I have every reason to commend your exactness in executing hitherto punctually whatever I have demanded, but now, if you have any regard for the lamp, your protector, you must show, if possible, more zeal and diligence than ever.

"I would have you build me, as soon as you can, a palace opposite, but at a proper distance from, the sultan's, fit to receive my spouse, the Princess Buddir al Buddoor. I leave the choice of the materials to you, that is to say, porphyry, jasper, agate, lapis lazuly, or the finest marble of various colours; and also the architecture of the building. But I expect that on the terraced roof of this palace you will build me a large hall crowned with a dome, and having four equal fronts, and that instead of layers of bricks, the walls be formed of gold and silver, laid alternately; that each front shall contain six windows, the lattices of all which shall be so enriched in the most tasteful workmanship with diamonds, rubies and emeralds that they shall exceed everything of the kind ever seen in the world. I would have an inner and outer court in front of the palace, and a spacious garden; but above all things, take care that there be laid in a place which you shall point out to me a treasure of gold and silver coin."

By the time Aladdin had instructed the genie respecting the building of his palace, the sun was set The next morning the genie presented himself and said, "Sir, your palace is finished; come and see how you like it." Aladdin had no sooner signified his consent than the genie transported him thither in an instant, and he found it so much

beyond his expectation that he could not sufficiently
admire it. The genie led him through all the
apartments, where he met with nothing but what
was rich and magnificent, with officers and slaves
all habited according to their rank and the services to which they were appointed The genie
then showed him the treasury, which was opened
by a treasurer, where Aladdin saw heaps of purses,
of different sizes, piled up to the top of the ceiling,
and disposed in most excellent order. The genie
assured him of the treasurer's fidelity, and thence
led him to the stables, where he showed him some
of the finest horses in the world, and the grooms
busy in dressing them; from thence they went to
the store-houses, which were filled with all things
necessary both for food and ornament.

When Aladdin had examined the palace from
top to bottom, and particularly the hall with the
four-and-twenty windows, and found it much beyond
whatever he could have imagined, he said, "Genie,
no one can be better satisfied than I am; and
indeed I should be much to blame if I found any
fault. There is only one thing wanting, which I
forgot to mention; that is, to lay from the sultan's
palace to the door of the apartment designed for
the princess, a carpet of fine velvet for her to
walk upon." The genie immediately disappeared,
and Aladdin saw what he desired executed in an
instant. The genie then returned and carried him

home before the gates of the sultan's palace were
opened.

When the porters, who had always been used
to an open prospect, came to open the gates, they
were amazed to find it obstructed, and to see a
carpet of velvet spread from the grand entrance.
They did not immediately look how far it extended,
but when they could discern Aladdin's palace distinctly, their surprise was increased. The news
of so extraordinary a wonder was presently spread
through the palace. The grand vizier, who arrived
soon after the gates were open, being no less
amazed than others at this novelty, ran and acquainted
the sultan, but endeavoured to make him believe
it to be all enchantment.

"Vizier," replied the sultan, "why will you
have it to be enchantment? You know, as well
as I, that it must be Aladdin's palace, which I
gave him leave to build for the reception of my
daughter After the proof we have had of his
riches, can we think it strange that he should raise
a palace in so short a time? He wished to surprise us, and let us see what wonders are to be
done with money in only one night. Confess sin-
cerely that the enchantment you talk of proceeds
from a little envy on account of your son's disappointment."

The hour of going to council put an end to
the conversation.

When Aladdin had been conveyed home and had dismissed the genie, he found his mother up and dressing herself in one of the suits he had ordered the genie to bring her. By the time the sultan rose from the council Aladdin had prepared his mother to go to the palace with her slaves, and desired her, if she saw the sultan, to tell him she should do herself the honour to attend the princess towards evening to her palace.

Aladdin's mother was received in the palace with honour, and introduced into the Princess Buddir al Buddoor's apartment by the chief of the guards. As soon as the princess saw her she rose, saluted, and desired her to sit down on a sofa; and while her women finished dressing and adorning her with the jewels which Aladdin had presented to her, a collation was served up. At the same time the sultan, who wished to be as much with his daughter as possible before he parted with her, came in and paid the old lady great respect.

When it was night the princess took her leave of the sultan her father; their adieus were tender and accompanied with tears. They embraced each other several times, and at last the princess left her own apartment for Aladdin's palace, with his mother on her left hand carried in a superb litter, followed by a hundred women slaves dressed with surprising magnificence. All the bands of music, which had played from the time Aladdin's mother

had arrived, being joined together, led the pro-
cession, followed by a hundred state ushers and
the like number of black chamberlains, in two files,
with their officers at their head   Four hundred of
the sultan's young pages carried flambeaux on each
side, which, together with the illuminations of the
sultan's and Aladdin's palaces, made it as light
as day.

At length the princess arrived at the new
palace. Aladdin ran with all imaginable joy to
receive her at the grand entrance. His mother
had taken care to point him out to the princess,
in the midst of the officers who surrounded him,
and she was charmed with his person   "Adorable
princess," said he, saluting her respectfully, as
soon as she had entered her apartment, "if I
have the misfortune to have displeased you by my
boldness in aspiring to the possession of so lovely
a princess, and my sultan's daughter, I must tell
you that you ought to blame your bright eyes and
charms, not me."

"Prince (as I may now call you)," answered the
princess, "I am obedient to the will of my father;
and it is enough for me to have seen you to tell
you that I obey without reluctance."

Aladdin, charmed with so agreeable and satis-
factory an answer, would not keep the princess
standing, but took her by the hand, which he kissed
with the greatest demonstration of joy, and led her

into a large hall, illuminated with an infinite number of wax candles, where, by the care of the genie, a noble feast was served up.

Aladdin led the princess to the place appointed for her, and during the repast a band of most harmonious instruments began a concert which lasted without intermission to the end of the repast

When the supper was ended there entered a company of dancers who performed, according to the custom of the country, several figure dances. And thus with feasting, singing and dancing the marriage festivities of Aladdin and Princess Buddir al Buddoor closed

Neither the princess nor the sultan her father had any reason to complain of Aladdin's behaviour as a husband. He was loving and courteous to his bride, generous and noble towards the populace, who loved him, and soon showed that he had a wise head in council and a courageous heart in battle. So the sultan had no fear but that when the time came for him to retire from the throne Aladdin would occupy it most worthily in his stead.

Aladdin had conducted himself in this manner several years, when the African magician, who undesignedly had been the instrument of raising him to so high a pitch of prosperity, recalled him to his recollection in Africa, whither he had returned after his expedition. And though he was almost

persuaded that Aladdin must have died miserably
in the subterranean abode where he had left him,
he formed a horoscope by which, when he came
to examine it, he found that Aladdin, instead of
dying in the cave, had made his escape, lived splen-
didly, was in possession of the wonderful lamp,
had married a princess, and was much honoured
and respected.

The magician's face became inflamed with anger,
and he cried out in a rage, "This sorry tailor's
son has discovered the secret and virtue of the
lamp! I believed his death to be certain, but find
that he enjoys the fruit of my labour and study!
I will, however, prevent his enjoying it long, or
perish in the attempt." He was not a great while
deliberating on what he should do, but the next
morning mounted a barb, set forwards, and never
stopped, but to refresh himself and horse, till he
arrived at the capital of China.

His first object was to enquire what people
said of Aladdin, and, taking a walk through the
town, he went to the most public and frequented
places where persons of the best distinction met.
He soon heard Aladdin's name spoken in tones of
respect and admiration and he took an early opportunity of enquiring who this Aladdin might be
of whom everyone was speaking "From whence
come you?" said the person he addressed himself to; "you must certainly be a stranger not to

have heard of Prince Aladdin and his wonderful palace."

"Forgive my ignorance," replied the African magician, "I arrived here but yesterday, and came from the farthest part of Africa, where the fame of his palace had not reached when I came away. The business which brought me hither was so urgent that my sole object was to arrive as soon as I could, without stopping anywhere, or making any acquaintance. But I will go immediately and satisfy my curiosity, if you will do me the favour to show me the way thither."

The person having pointed out the way, the African magician went thither instantly. When he came to the palace, and had examined it on all sides, he doubted not but that Aladdin had made use of the lamp to build it.

The next point was to ascertain where the lamp was whether Aladdin carried it about with him, or where he kept it; and this he was to discover by an operation of geomancy. As soon as he entered his lodging, he took his square box of sand, which he always carried with him when he travelled, and after he had performed some operations, he found that the lamp was in Aladdin's palace, and so great was his joy at the discovery that he could hardly contain himself. "Well," said he, "I shall have the lamp, and I defy Aladdin's preventing my carrying it off, and making him sink

to his original meanness, from which he has taken
so high a flight."

On his return to the khan at which he was
staying he entered into conversation with the keeper
of it, and after expatiating upon the beauties of
Aladdin's wonderful palace, declared that he had
the greatest curiosity to behold the owner of so
much magnificence.

"That will be no difficult matter," replied the
master of the khan, "you may see him any day
when he is in town, but at present he is not at
the palace, but has gone these three days on a
hunting expedition, which is to last eight days."

The magician thought this too good an opportunity to neglect. He went to a coppersmith and
bought a dozen handsome copper lamps which he
put into a basket, and hanging the basket on his
arm, he set out for Aladdin's palace. As he
approached it he began crying. "Who will change
old lamps for new ones?" A crowd of children
collected who hooted, and thought him, as did all
who chanced to be passing by, a madman or a
fool, to offer to change new lamps for old ones.
The magician paid no heed to the scoffing and
laughter, but continued his cry, "Who will change
old lamps for new?"

He repeated this so often, walking backwards
and forwards in front of the palace, that the
princess, who was then in the hall with the four-

and-twenty windows, hearing a man cry something, and not being able to distinguish his words, owing to the hooting of the children and increasing mob about him, sent one of her women slaves to know what he cried

The slave was not long before she returned, and ran into the hall, laughing heartily. "Well,

giggler," said the princess, "will you tell me what you laugh at?" "Madam," answered the slave, laughing still, "who can forbear laughing, to see a fool with a basket on his arm, full of fine new lamps, asking to change them for old ones; the children and mob crowd about him so that he can hardly stir, making all the noise they can in derision of him."

"Who will change old lamps for new?"

Another female slave hearing this, said, "Now you speak of lamps, I know not whether the princess may have observed it, but there is an old one upon a shelf of the princes robing room, and whoever owns it will not be sorry to find a new one in its stead. If the princess chooses, she may have the pleasure of trying if this fool is so silly as to give a new lamp for an old one without taking anything for the exchange"

The lamp this slave spoke of was the wonderful lamp, which Aladdin had laid upon the shelf
before he departed for the chase; this he had done
several times before, but neither the princess, the
slaves nor the chamberlains had ever taken notice
of it At all other times except when hunting he
carried it about his person.

The princess, who knew not the value of this
lamp, and the interest that Aladdin, not to mention
herself, had to keep it safe, entered into the plea-
santry, and commanded a chamberlain to take it and
make the exchange. The chamberlain obeyed, went
out of the hall, and no sooner got to the palace
gates than he saw the African magician, called to
him, and, showing him the old lamp, said, "Give
me a new lamp for this."

The magician never doubted but this was the
lamp he wanted. There could be no other such
in the palace, where every utensil was gold or
silver. He snatched it eagerly out of the chamberlain's hand, and thrusting it as far as he could into
his breast, offered him his basket, and bade him
choose which he liked best. The chamberlain picked
out one and carried it to the princess.

As for the magician, having obtained what he
wanted, he threw away the rest of his new lamps,
hastened out of the town, and never waited until
he had reached a lonely spot at some distance
from the wonderful palace; then he drew the lamp

from his breast and rubbed it. At that summons the genie appeared and said, "What would you have? I am ready to obey you as your slave, and the slave of all those who have that lamp in their hands; both I and the other slaves of the lamp."

A female slave.

"I command you," replied the magician, "to transport me immediately, and the palace which you and the other slaves of the lamp have built in this city, with all the people in it, to Africa."

The genie made no reply, but with the assistance of the other genii, the slaves of the lamp, immediately transported him and the palace entire to the spot whither he was desired to convey it.

As soon as the sultan rose the next morning, according to custom, he went into his closet to have the pleasure of contemplating and admiring Aladdin's palace. When he first looked that way, and instead of a palace saw an empty space such as it was before the palace was built, he thought he was mistaken, and rubbed his eyes; but when he looked again, he still saw nothing. He looked again in front, to the right and left, but beheld nothing more than he had formerly been used to

see from his window. His amazement was so great
that he stood for some time turning his eyes to
the spot where the palace had stood, but where
it was no longer to be seen. He could not comprehend how so large a palace as Aladdin's, which
he had seen plainly every day for some years, and
but the day before, should vanish so soon, without
leaving so much as a stone behind

"Certainly," said he to himself, "I am not
mistaken, it stood there. if it had fallen, the
materials would have lain in heaps, and if it had
been swallowed up by an earthquake there would
be some mark left." At last he retired to his
apartment, not without looking behind him before
he quitted the spot, ordered the grand vizier to
be sent for with expedition, and in the meantime
sat down, his mind agitated by so many different
conjectures that he knew not what to resolve.

The grand vizier came with so much precipitation that neither he nor his attendants, as they
passed, missed Aladdin's palace; neither did the
porters when they opened the palace gates observe
any alteration.

When he came into the sultan's presence he
said to him, "The haste in which your Majesty
sent for me makes me believe something extraordinary has happened, since you know this is a
day of public audience, and I should not have
failed of attending at the usual time."

"Indeed," said the sultan, "it is something very extraordinary, as you say, and you will allow it to be so: tell me what is become of Aladdin's palace."

"His palace!" replied the grand vizier, in amazement, "I thought as I passed it stood in its

usual place; such substantial buildings are not so easily removed." "Go into my closet," said the sultan, "and tell me if you can see it."

The grand vizier went into the closet, where he was struck with no less amazement than the sultan had been. When he was well assured that there was not the least appearance of this palace, he returned to the sultan. "Well," said

The grand vizier.

the sultan, "have you seen Aladdin's palace?" "No," answered the vizier, "but your Majesty may remember that I had the honour to tell you that palace, which was the subject of your admiration, with all its immense riches, was only the work of magic and a magician; but your Majesty would not pay the least attention to what I said."

The sultan, who could not deny what the grand

vizier had represented to him, flew into the greater
passion "Where is that impostor, that wicked
wretch?" said he, "that I may have his head taken
off immediately." "Sir," replied the grand vizier,
"it is some days since he came to take his leave
of your Majesty, on pretence of hunting, he ought
to be sent for, to tell us what is become of his
palace."

"Command a detachment of horse to bring him
to me loaded with chains," said the sultan. The
grand vizier gave the order and instructed the officer
in command how he should act, that Aladdin might
not escape. Accordingly about five or six leagues
from the town he was met returning from the
chase The officer advanced respectfully and informed him the sultan was so impatient to see
him that he had sent his party to accompany him
home.

Aladdin had not the least suspicion of the true
reason of their meeting him; but when he came
within half a league of the city, the detachment
surrounded him, when the officer addressed himself
to him and said, "Prince, it is with great regret
that I declare to you the sultan's order to arrest
you, and to carry you before him as a criminal.
I beg of you not to take it ill that we acquit
ourselves of our duty, and to forgive us "

Aladdin, who knew himself to be innocent, was
much surprised at this declaration, and asked the

officer of what crime he was accused. To this the
officer was unable to reply, and Aladdin, seeing it
was useless to resist, alighted from his horse, and
said : "Execute your orders; I am not conscious that

Aladdin was obliged to follow him on foot.

I have committed any offence against the sultan's
person or government."

A heavy chain was immediately put about his
neck, and fastened round his body, so that both
his arms were pinioned down ; the officer then put
himself at the head of the detachment, and one
of the troopers, taking hold of the end of the

chain and proceeding after the officer, led Aladdin, who was obliged to follow him on foot, into the city.

When this detachment entered the suburbs, the people, who saw Aladdin thus led as a state criminal, never doubted but that his head was to be cut off, and as he was generally beloved, some took sabres and other arms, and those who had none gathered stones, and followed the escort.

No sooner was Aladdin brought before the sultan than the executioner was summoned and received orders to strike off the prisoner's head immediately; but at that instant the grand vizier, perceiving that the populace had forced the guard of horse, crowded the great square before the palace, and were scaling the walls in several places, and beginning to pull them down to force their way in, said to the sultan, "I beg of your Majesty to consider what you are going to do, since you will hazard your palace being destroyed, and who knows what fatal consequence may follow?"

"My palace forced!" replied the sultan; "who can have that audacity?"

"Sir," answered the grand vizier, "if your Majesty will but cast your eyes towards the great square, and on the palace walls, you will perceive the truth of what I say."

The sultan was so much alarmed when he saw so great a crowd and how enraged they were that he ordered the executioner to put his sabre immediately into the scabbard, to unbind Aladdin, and at the same time commanded the porters to declare to the people that the sultan had pardoned him, and that they might retire

Those who had already got upon the walls, and were witnesses of what had passed, abandoned their design and got quickly down, overjoyed that they had saved the life of a man they dearly loved, and published the news amongst the rest. The justice which the sultan had done to Aladdin soon disarmed the populace of their rage; the tumult abated, and the mob dispersed

When Aladdin found himself at liberty, he turned towards the balcony, and, perceiving the sultan, raised his voice, and said to him in a moving manner, "I beg of your Majesty to add one favour more to that which I have already received, which is, to let me know my crime.'

"Your crime," answered the sultan, "perfidious wretch! Do you not know it? Come hither, and I will show it you"

Aladdin went up to the sultan, who went before him and led him into his room. When he came to the door, he said "Go in, you ought to know whereabouts your palace stood, look round and tell me what has become of it."

Aladdin looked, but saw nothing. He perceived the spot upon which his palace had stood, but, not being able to divine how it had disappeared, was thrown into such great confusion and amazement that he could not return one word of answer.

The sultan growing impatient, demanded of him "Where is your palace, and what has become of my daughter?" Aladdin, breaking silence, replied "Sir, I perceive and own that the palace which I have built is not in its place, but is vanished; neither can I tell your Majesty where it may be, but can assure you I had no concern in its removal"

"I am not so much concerned about your palace," replied the sultan, "I value my daughter ten thousand times more, and would have you find her out, otherwise I will cause your head to be struck off, and no consideration shall divert me from my purpose."

"I beg of your Majesty," answered Aladdin, "to grant me forty days to make my enquiries, and if in that time I have not the success I wish, I will offer my head at the foot of your throne, to be disposed of at your pleasure."

"I give you the forty days you ask," said the sultan, "but think not to abuse the favour I show you, by imagining you shall escape my resentment; for I will find you out in whatsoever part of the world you may conceal yourself."

Aladdin went out of the sultan's presence with great humiliation, and in a condition worthy of pity.

He wandered away, far from the sultan's Court

and all those who had known him in his days of prosperity, and found himself at length by the river's brink. Possessed by despair, he determined to put an end to his existence, but first, being a good Mussulman, he wished to say his prayers. He went to the river's brink to wash himself, as is the custom with Mussulmen before praying, but, the place being steep and slippery, he slid down and would have fallen had he not caught at a projecting rock. Happily for him he still had on the ring which the African magician had put on his finger before he went down into the subterranean abode to fetch the precious lamp. In slipping down the bank he rubbed the ring so hard that immediately the same genie appeared whom he had seen in the cave.

"What would you have?" said the genie, "I am ready to obey you as your slave, and the slave of all those who have that ring on their finger; both I and the other slaves of the ring."

Aladdin, agreeably surprised at an apparition he so little expected in his present calamity, replied: "Save my life, genie, a second time, either by showing me to the place where the palace I caused to be built now stands, or immediately transporting it back where it first stood."

"What you command me," answered the genie, "is not wholly in my power; I am only the slave of the ring; you must address yourself to the slave of the lamp."

12

"If that be the case," replied Aladdin, "I
command you, by the power of the ring, to transport me to the spot where my palace stands, in
what part of the world soever it may be, and set
me down under the window of the Princess Buddir
al Buddoor."

These words were no sooner out of his mouth,
than the genie transported him into Africa, to the
midst of a large plain where his palace stood, at
no great distance from a city, and placing him
exactly under the window of the princess's apartment, left him. All this was done almost in an
instant.

Aladdin, notwithstanding the darkness of the
night, knew his palace and the Princess Buddir al
Buddoor's apartments again; but as the night was
far advanced, and all was quiet in the palace, he
retired to some distance, and sat down at the foot
of a large tree. There, full of hopes and reflecting
on his happiness, for which he was indebted to
chance, he found himself in a much more comfort-
able situation than when he was arrested and
carried before the sultan, being now delivered
from the immediate danger of losing his life. He
amused himself for some time with these agreeable
thoughts, but, not having slept for two days, was
not able to resist the drowsiness which came upon
him, but fell fast asleep.

The next morning, as soon as day dawned,

Aladdin rose and went towards the apartments where he expected to find his dear Princess Buddir al Buddoor. As he walked he began to consider with himself whence the cause of this misfortune had proceeded, and, after mature reflection, no longer doubted that it was owing to having trusted the lamp out of his sight. He accused himself of negligence in letting it be a moment away from him. But what puzzled him most was, that he could not imagine who had been so envious of his happiness. He would soon have guessed this if he had known that both he and the palace were in Africa, the very name of which would soon have made him remember the magician, his declared enemy, but the genie, the slave of the ring, had not made the least mention of the name of the country, nor had Aladdin enquired.

The princess rose earlier that morning than she had done since her transportation into Africa by the magician, whose presence she was forced to support once a day, because he was master of the palace; but she had always treated him so scornfully that he dared not reside in it. As she was dressing, one of the women, looking through the window, perceived Aladdin, and instantly told her mistress. The princess, who could not believe the joyful tidings, hastened herself to the window, and, seeing Aladdin, immediately opened it. The noise of opening the window made Aladdin turn his head that way, and perceiving the princess he saluted her with an air that expressed his joy.

There was a little private door just beneath the princess's window, and Aladdin entered at this and soon afterwards held his dear princess in his arms. After the first rapture of reunion, he said to her "Before we speak of anything else, tell me what has become of an old lamp which I left upon a shelf in my robing chamber when I left for the chase."

"Alas! dear husband," answered the princess, "I was afraid our misfortune might be owing to that lamp; and what grieves me most is that I have been the cause of it."

"Princess," replied Aladdin, "do not blame yourself, since it was entirely my fault, for I ought to have taken more care of it. But let us now think only of repairing the loss; tell me what has happened, and into whose hands it has fallen."

The princess then related how she had changed the old lamp for a new one, which she ordered to be fetched, that he might see it, and how the next morning she found herself in the unknown country they were then in, which she was told was Africa by the traitor who had transported her thither by his magic art.

"Princess," said Aladdin, interrupting her, "you have informed me who the traitor is, by telling me we are in Africa. He is the most perfidious of

Aladdin saluted her with an air that expressed his joy.

men; but this is neither a time nor place to give you a full account of his villainies. I desire you only to tell me what he has done with the lamp, and where he has put it."

"He carries it carefully wrapt up in his bosom," said the princess; "and this I can assure you because he pulled it out before me, and showed it to me in triumph."

"Princess," said Aladdin, "do not be displeased that I trouble you with so many questions, since they are equally important to us both. But to come to what most particularly concerns me; tell me, I conjure you, how so wicked and perfidious a man treats you."

"Since I have been here," replied the princess, "he repairs once every day to see me, and to try and persuade me to take him for my husband, assuring me that you were dead."

Aladdin then told the princess that it would be necessary for him to leave her for a time, in order to carry out a plan he had formed to rescue both of them from the power of the wicked magician.

"I shall return by noon," said he, "and will then communicate my design to you and tell you what you must do to ensure success. But that you may not be surprised, I think it proper to acquaint you that I shall change my apparel, and beg of you to give orders that I may not wait long at the private door, but that it may be opened

at the first knock." All which the princess promised to observe.

When Aladdin was out of the palace, he looked
round him on all sides, and perceiving a peasant
going into the country, hastened after him, and,
when he had overtaken him, made a proposal to
him to change habits, which the man agreed to.
When they had made the exchange, the country-
man went about his business, and Aladdin to the
city, and entering a druggist's shop asked for a
certain powder.

The druggist, judging Aladdin by his habit to
be very poor, and that he had not money enough
to pay for it, told him he had it, but that it was
very dear; upon which Aladdin, penetrating his
thoughts, pulled out his purse and, showing him
some gold, asked for half a dram of the powder,
which the druggist weighed, wrapped up in a paper,
and gave him, telling him the price was a piece
of gold. Aladdin put the money into his hand
and, staying no longer in the town than just to
get a little refreshment, returned to the palace,
where he was not kept long at the private door.

As soon as he was in the princess's apartment
he disclosed his plan to her. He bade her, however distasteful it might be to her, to dissemble
a little when the magician visited her, and pretend
that she was no longer so averse to him, and that
she was beginning to forget Aladdin.

She was to invite the magician to sup with her and tell him she would be glad to taste some of the wines of his country, which he would be sure to go and fetch.

"During his absence," said Aladdin, "put this powder into one of the cups you are accustomed to drink out of and, setting it by, charge the slave you may order that night to attend you, on a signal you shall agree upon, to bring that cup to you When the magician and you have eaten and drunk as much as you choose, let her bring you the cup, and then change cups with him. He will esteem it so great a favour that he will not refuse, but eagerly quaff it off; but no sooner will he have drunk, than you will see him fall backwards."

The princess having arranged to carry out these instructions, Aladdin then took his leave, and the princess charged her women to dress her in her most gorgeous attire. This they did and shortly afterwards the magician arrived.

As soon as he entered the great hall where the princess waited to receive him, she rose with an enchanting grace and smile, and pointed with her hand to the most honourable place, waiting till he sat down, that she might sit at the same time, which was a civility she had never shown him before

The African magician, dazzled more with the lustre of the princess's eyes than the glittering of the jewels with which she was adorned, was much surprised The smiling and graceful air with which she received him, so opposite to her former behaviour, had quite fascinated his heart.

When he was seated, the princess, to free him from his embarrassment, broke silence first, looking at him all the time in such a manner as to make him believe that he was not so odious to her as she had given him to understand hitherto, and said. "You are doubtless amazed to find me so much altered to-day; but your surprise will not be so great when I acquaint you that I am naturally of a disposition so opposite to melancholy and grief, sorrow and uneasiness, that I always strive to put them as far away as possible. Having heard from you of Aladdin's fate, I have reflected that all my tears cannot recall him, and have therefore decided to grieve no more. If you will bear me company to-night I will order supper to be prepared at once; I have in this palace no wines except those of China, and I have a great desire to taste those of this country, and doubt not you will be able to procure me some "

"I have," said the magician, "a flagon of wine seven years old, and it is not too much to say it is the finest in the world I will go and fetch it and will return again immediately."

The African magician, full of hopes of his expected happiness, rather flew than ran, and returned quickly with the wine The princess, not doubting but he would make haste, put with her own hand the powder Aladdin had given her into the cup set apart for that purpose. They sat down at the table opposite to each other.

After they had eaten for some time, the princess called for some wine, drank the magician's health, and afterwards said to him· "Indeed, you had a full right to commend your wine, since I never tasted any so delicious."

"Charming princess," said he, holding in his hand the cup which had been presented to him, "my wine becomes more exquisite by your approbation "

When they had each drunk two or three cups more, the princess, who had completely charmed the African magician by her civility and obliging behaviour, gave the signal to the slave who served them with wine, bidding her bring the cup which had been filled for herself, and at the same time bring the magician a full goblet. When they both had their cups in their hands, she said to him, "I know not how you express your loves in these parts when drinking together. With us in China the lover and his mistress exchange cups, and drink each other's health;" at the same time she presented to him the cup which was in her hand, and held out her hand to receive his. He hastened to make the exchange, saying "Indeed, Princess, we

Africans are not so refined in the art of love as
you Chinese."

With that he set the cup to his lips and
drained it to the very last drop, when immediately
his eyes began to roll in his head and he fell
backwards, lifeless, on the sofa.

The princess had no occasion to order the
private door to be opened to Aladdin, for her
women were so disposed from the great hall to
the foot of the staircase, that the word was no
sooner given that the African magician was fallen
backwards, than the door was immediately opened.

As soon as Aladdin entered the hall, he saw
the magician stretched backwards on the sofa. The
princess rose from her seat, and ran overjoyed to
embrace him, but he stopped her, and said: "Princess, it is not yet time; oblige me by retiring to
your apartment, and let me be left alone a moment,
while I endeavour to transport you back to China
as speedily as you were brought from thence."

When the princess, her women and guards
were gone out of the hall, Aladdin shut the door,
and going directly to the dead body of the magician, opened his vest, took out the lamp, which
was carefully wrapped up, as the princess had told
him, and unfolding and rubbing it, the genie immediately appeared.

"Genie," said Aladdin, "I have called to
command you, on the part of your good mistress

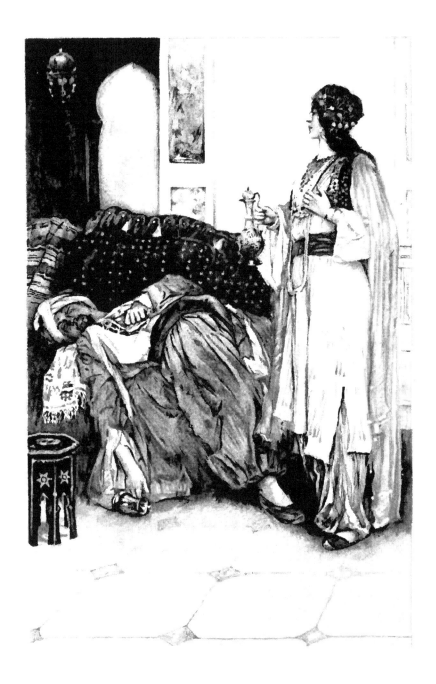

the lamp, to transport this palace instantly into China, to the place from whence it was brought hither."

The genie bowed his head in token of obedience, and disappeared. Immediately the palace was transported into China, and its removal was only felt by two little shocks, the one when it was lifted up, the other when it was set down, and both in a very short interval of time.

Aladdin hastened to the princess's apartment and embraced her tenderly, but as it was very late by this time they retired to rest without first visiting the sultan.

From the time of the transportation of Aladdin's palace, the princess's father had been inconsolable for the loss of her. Before the disaster he used to go every morning into his closet to please himself with viewing the palace; he went now many times in the day to renew his tears, and plunge himself into the deepest melancholy, by the idea of no more seeing that which once gave him so much pleasure, and reflecting how he had lost what was most dear to him in this world.

The very morning of the return of Aladdin's palace, the sultan went, by break of day, into his closet to indulge his sorrows. Absorbed in himself, and in a pensive mood, he cast his eyes towards the spot, expecting only to see an open space; but perceiving the vacancy filled up he looked again more attentively, and was convinced beyond the power of doubt that it was his son-in-law's palace. Joy and gladness succeeded to sorrow and grief. He returned immediately into his apartment, and ordered a horse to be saddled and brought to him without delay, which he mounted that instant, thinking he could not make haste enough to the palace.

Aladdin, who foresaw what would happen, rose that morning by daybreak, put on one of the most magnificent habits his wardrobe afforded, and went up into the hall of twenty-four windows, from whence he perceived the sultan approaching, and got down soon enough to receive him at the foot of the great staircase, and to help him to dismount. "Aladdin," said the sultan, "I cannot speak to you till I have seen and embraced my daughter."

He led the sultan into the princess's apartment. The happy father embraced her with his face bathed in tears of joy, and the princess, on her side, showed him all the testimonies of the extreme pleasure the sight of him afforded her.

He then enquired anxiously as to the method by which so large a palace had been transported so quickly from one place to another.

"Aladdin had no concern in it," said the princess; "I was myself the innocent cause of it"

To persuade the sultan of the truth of what she said, she gave him a full account of how the

African magician had disguised himself, and offered to change new lamps for old ones; how she had amused herself in making the exchange, being en-

"Aladdin, I cannot speak to you until I have seen my daughter."

tirely ignorant of the secret and importance of the wonderful lamp; how the palace and herself were carried away and transported into Africa, with the African magician, who was recognised by two of her women and the chamberlain who made the exchange of the lamp

She also told the sultan of her meeting with Aladdin and how he had compassed the wicked magician's death. "The rest of the story," said she, "I leave to Aladdin to recount"

Aladdin thereupon took up the story and, having described the means by which he had recovered the magic lamp and transported the palace to China, invited the sultan to accompany him to the great hall and see the magician lying punished as he deserved.

The sultan rose instantly and went into the hall, where he saw the magician lying dead as Aladdin had described.

Thus had Aladdin once more escaped from the danger of losing his life, but before long he was again in peril

The African magician had a younger brother, who was equally skilful as a necromancer, and even surpassed him in villainy and pernicious designs. As they did not live together, or in the same city, they failed not every year to inform themselves, by their art, each where the other resided, and whether they stood in need of one another's assistance.

Some time after the African magician had failed in his enterprise against Aladdin, his younger brother, who had heard no tidings of him, and was not in Africa, but in a distant country, had the wish to know in what part of the world he sojourned, the state of his health, and what he was doing, he had recourse to his magic and found to his surprise that his brother was no longer living, but had been poisoned by a person of mean birth who had married a princess, and who was living in the capital of China.

The magician's brother lost no time in useless regrets, which could not restore him to life, but resolved to immediately avenge his death, and set out at once for the capital of China.

When he arrived there he took a lodging, and soon afterwards walked through the city, visiting the places of public amusement and spots most frequented. Here he listened to the converse around him and heard some persons speaking of the piety and virtue of a woman called Fatima

As he fancied that this woman might be serviceable to him in the project he had conceived, he took one of the company aside, and requested to be informed more particularly who that holy woman was, and what sort of miracles she performed.

"What!" said the person whom he addressed, "have you never seen or heard of her? She is the admiration of the whole town, for her fasting, her austerities, and her exemplary life. Except Mondays and Fridays, she never stirs out of her little cell, and on those days on which she comes into the town, she does an infinite deal of good; for there is

13

not a person that has the headache but is cured by her laying her hand upon them."

The magician wanted no further information. He only asked the person in what part of the town this holy woman's cell was situated. After he had informed himself on this head, he determined on the detestable design of murdering her and assuming her character.

When night fell he went straight to Fatima's cell, opened the door, which was only fastened with a latch, and shut it again after he had entered, without any noise. When he entered the cell, he perceived Fatima by moonlight lying asleep on a sofa. He awakened her, and clapped a dagger to her breast.

The pious Fatima, opening her eyes, was much surprised to see a man with a dagger at her heart ready to stab her, and who said to her, "If you cry out, or make the least noise, I will kill you, but get up, and do as I shall direct you."

Fatima, who had lain down in her habit, got up, trembling with fear. "Do not be so much frightened," said the magician, "I only want your habit, give it to me and take mine." Accordingly Fatima and he changed clothes. He then said to her. "Colour my face, that I may be like you;" but perceiving that the poor creature could not help trembling, to encourage her he said, "I tell you again, you need not fear anything; I will not take away your life."

Fatima lighted her lamp, led him into the cell, and, dipping a soft brush into a certain liquor, rubbed it over his face, assured him the colour would not change, and that his face was of the same hue as her own : after which she put her own head-dress on his head, also a veil, with which she showed him

The magician entered the cell.

how to hide his face as he passed through the town. After this, she put a long string of beads about his neck, which hung down to the middle of his body, and giving him the stick she used to walk with in his hand, brought him a looking-glass, and bade him look if he was not as like her as possible. The

13*

magician found himself disguised as he wished, but he did not keep his promise, for he at once proceeded to kill her and then threw her body into a well.

The magician, thus disguised like the holy woman Fatima, spent the remainder of the night in the cell. The next morning, two hours after sunrise, though it was not a day the holy woman used to go out on, he crept out of the cell, being well persuaded that nobody would ask him any questions; or, if they should, he had an answer ready for them.

As soon as the people saw the holy woman, as they imagined him to be, they presently gathered about him in a great crowd. Some begged his blessing, others kissed his hand, and others, more reserved, only the hem of his garment; while others, whether their heads ached, or they wished to be preserved against that disorder, stooped for him to lay his hands upon them, which he did, muttering some words in form of prayer, and, in short, counterfeited so well that everybody took him for the holy woman.

After frequently stopping to satisfy people of this description he came at last to the square before Aladdin's palace. The crowd was so great that the eagerness to get at him increased in proportion. Those who were the most zealous and strong forced their way through the crowd. There were such quarrels, and so great a noise, that the princess, who was in the hall of four-and-twenty windows, heard it, and asked what was the matter; but nobody being able to give her an answer, she ordered them to enquire and inform her. One of her women looked out of the window, and then told her it was a great crowd of people collected about the holy woman to be cured of the headache.

The princess, who had long heard of this holy woman, but had never seen her, was very desirous to have some conversation with her, which the chief of the guards perceiving, told her it was an easy matter to bring her to her, if she desired and commanded it; and the princess expressing her wishes, he immediately sent four guards for the pretended holy woman.

As soon as the crowd saw the guards, they made way, and the magician, perceiving also that they were coming for him, advanced to meet them, overjoyed to find his plot proceeded so well. "Holy woman," said one of the guards, "the princess wishes to see you, and has sent us for you"

"The princess does me too great an honour," replied the false Fatima, "I am ready to obey her command," and at the same time followed the guards to the palace.

When the magician, who under a holy garment disguised a wicked heart, was introduced into the great hall and perceived the princess, he began a prayer, which contained a long enumeration of vows and good wishes for the princess's health and prosperity, and that she might have everything she desired.

When the pretended Fatima had finished his harangue, the princess said to him, "I thank you, good Mother, for your prayers; come and sit by me."

The false Fatima sat down with affected modesty; the princess, then resuming her discourse, said "My good Mother, I have one thing to request, which you must not refuse me; it is, to stay with me, that you may edify me with your way of living."

"Princess," said the counterfeit Fatima, "I beg of you not to ask what I cannot consent to without neglecting my prayers and devotion."

"That shall be no hindrance to you," answered the princess; "I have a great many apartments un-occupied; you shall choose which you like best, and have as much liberty to perform your devotions as if you were in your own cell."

The magician, who desired nothing more than to introduce himself into the palace, did not urge much to excuse himself from accepting the obliging offer which the princess made him.

"Princess," said he, "whatever resolution a poor wretched woman as I am may have made to re-nounce the pomp and grandeur of this world, I dare not presume to oppose the will and commands of so pious and charitable a princess."

Upon this the princess, rising up, said· "Come with me, I will show you what vacant apartments I have, that you may make choice of that you like best."

The magician followed the princess, and of all the apartments she showed him, with pretended humility made choice of that which was the worst furnished.

Afterwards the princess would have brought him back again into the great hall to make him dine with her; but considering that he should then be obliged to show his face, which he had always taken care to conceal, and fearing that the princess should find out that he was not Fatima, he begged of her earnestly to excuse him, telling her that he never ate anything but bread and dried fruits, and desiring to eat that slight repast in his own apartment. The princess granted his request, saying "You may be as free here, good Mother, as if you were in your own cell: I will order you a dinner, but remember I expect you as soon as you have finished your repast."

After the princess had dined, and the false Fatima had been informed by one of the chamberlains that she was risen from table, he failed not to wait upon her. "My good Mother," said the princess, "I am overjoyed to have the company of so holy a woman as yourself, who will confer a blessing upon this palace. But now I am speaking of the palace, pray how do you like it? And before I show it all to you, tell me first what you think of this hall."

Upon this question, the counterfeit Fatima, who, to act his part the better, affected to hang down his head, without so much as ever once lifting it, at last looked up, and surveyed the hall from one end to the other When he had examined it well, he said to the princess "As far as such a solitary being as I am, who am unacquainted with what the world calls beautiful, can judge, this hall is truly admirable and most beautiful; there wants but one thing."

"What is that, good Mother?" demanded the princess; "tell me, I conjure you! For my part, I always believed, and have heard say, it wanted nothing; but if it does, it shall be supplied"

"Princess," said the false Fatima, with great dissimulation, "forgive me the liberty I have taken, but my opinion is, if it can be of any importance, that if a roc's egg were hung up in the middle of the dome, this hall would have no parallel in the four quarters of the world, and your palace would be the wonder of the universe"

"My good Mother," said the princess, "what bird is a roc, and where may one get an egg?"

"Princess," replied the pretended Fatima, "it is a bird of prodigious size, which inhabits the summit of Mount Caucasus; the architect who built your palace can get you one."

After the princess had thanked the false Fatima for what she believed her good advice, she conversed with her upon other matters, but could not forget

the roc's egg, which she resolved to request of
Aladdin when he returned from hunting. He had
been gone six days, but he returned that evening
after the false Fatima had taken leave of the princess and retired to his apartment. As soon as he
arrived, he went directly to the princess's apartment,
saluted and embraced her, but she seemed to receive
him coldly.

"My Princess," said he, "I think you are not so
cheerful as you used to be, has anything happened
during my absence which has displeased you or
given you any trouble or dissatisfaction?"

"It is a trifling matter," replied the princess,
"which gives me so little concern that I could not
have thought you could have perceived it in my
countenance; but since you have unexpectedly discovered some alteration, I will no longer disguise
the matter from you

"I always believed," continued the princess,
"that our palace was the most superb, magnificent,
and complete in the world, but I will tell you now
what I find fault with, upon examining the hall of
four-and-twenty windows. Do not you think with
me, that it would be complete if a roc's egg were
hung up in the midst of the dome?"

"Princess," replied Aladdin, "it is enough that
you think there wants such an ornament, you shall
see, by the diligence used to supply that deficiency,
that there is nothing I would not do for your sake "

Aladdin left the Princess Buddir al Buddoor that moment, and went up into the hall of four-and-twenty windows, where, pulling out of his bosom the lamp, which, after the danger he had been exposed to, he always carried about with him, he rubbed it, upon which the genie immediately appeared

"Genie," said Aladdin, "I wish a roc's egg to be hung up in the midst of the dome; I command you, in the name of this lamp, to repair the deficiency."

Aladdin had no sooner pronounced these words, than the genie gave so loud and terrible a cry that the hall shook, and Aladdin could scarcely stand upright.

"What! wretch," said the genie, in a voice that would have made the most undaunted man tremble, "is it not enough that I and my companions have done everything for you, but you, by an unheard-of ingratitude must command me to bring my master, and hang him up in the midst of this dome? This attempt deserves that you, your wife, and your palace should be immediately reduced to ashes; but you are happy that the request does not come from yourself. Know then, that the true author is the brother of the African magician, your enemy, whom you have destroyed as he deserved. He is now in your palace, disguised in the habit of the holy woman Fatima, whom he has murdered; and it is he who has suggested to your wife to make this pernicious demand His design is to kill you, there-

"My dear husband, what have you done?"

fore take care of yourself." After these words, the genie disappeared.

Aladdin lost not a word of what the genie had said. He had heard talk of the holy woman Fatima, and how she pretended to cure the headache. He returned to the princess's apartment, and without mentioning a word of what had happened, sat down, and complained of a great pain which had suddenly seized his head; upon which the princess ordered the holy woman to be called, and then told Aladdin how she had invited her to the palace, and that she had appointed her an apartment.

When the pretended Fatima came, Aladdin said. "Come hither, good Mother, I am glad to see you here at so fortunate a time; I am tormented with a violent pain in my head, and request your assistance, and hope you will not refuse me that favour which you do to so many persons afflicted with this complaint."

So saying, he arose, but held down his head. The counterfeit Fatima advanced towards him, with his hand all the time on a dagger concealed in his girdle under his gown, which Aladdin observing, seized his hand before he had drawn it, and pierced him to the heart with his own dagger.

"My dear husband, what have you done?" cried the princess in surprise. "You have killed the holy woman."

"No, my princess," answered Aladdin with

emotion, "I have not killed Fatima, but a villain, who would have assassinated me if I had not prevented him. This wicked wretch," added he, uncovering his face, "has strangled Fatima, whom you accuse me of killing, and disguised himself in her clothes with intent to murder me but that you may know him better, he is brother to the African magician."

Aladdin then informed her how he came to know these particulars, and afterwards ordered the dead body to be taken away.

Thus was Aladdin delivered from the persecution of two brothers, who were magicians Within a few years afterwards, the sultan died in a good old age, and as he left no male children, the Princess Buddir al Buddoor, as lawful heir of the throne, and her husband, Aladdin, reigned together many years, and left a numerous and illustrious posterity.

ALI BABA.

Cassim's wife.

IN a town in Persia there lived two brothers, one named Cassim, the other Ali Baba. Their father left them scarcely anything; what there was he wished to be divided equally between them, and it therefore seemed as though their fortune ought to have been equal; but chance determined otherwise.

Cassim married a wife who soon after became heiress to a large sum of money and a warehouse full of rich goods, so that he all at once became one of the richest and most considerable merchants, and lived at his ease.

Ali Baba, on the other hand, who had married a woman as poor as himself, lived in a very wretched habitation, and had no other means to maintain his wife and children but his daily labour of cutting wood, and bringing it upon three asses, which were his whole substance, to town to sell.

One day, when Ali Baba was in the forest,
and had just cut wood enough to load his asses,
he saw at a distance a great cloud of dust, which
seemed to be driven towards him; he observed it
very attentively, and distinguished soon after a body
of horsemen Though there had been no rumour
of robbers in that country, Ali Baba began to
think that they might prove such, and without
considering what might become of his asses, resolved
to save himself He climbed up a large, thick
tree, whose branches, at a little distance from the
ground, were so close to one another that there
was but little space between them He placed
himself in the middle, from whence he could see
all that passed without being discovered, and the
tree stood at the base of a rock, so steep and
craggy that nobody could climb it

The horsemen, who were all well mounted
and armed, came to the foot of this rock, and
there dismounted Ali Baba counted forty of them,
and from their looks and equipage was assured
that they were robbers. Nor was he mistaken in
his opinion, for they were a troop of banditti, who,
without doing any harm in the neighbourhood,
robbed at a distance, and made that place their
rendezvous Ali Baba watched every man un-
bridle his horse, tie him to a shrub, and hang
about his neck a bag of corn. Then each of them
took his saddle wallet, which seemed to Ali Baba

to be full of gold and silver from its weight. One, whom he took to be their captain, came with his wallet on his back under the tree in which Ali Baba was concealed, and, making his way through some shrubs, pronounced these words, so distinctly that Ali Baba overheard him : "Open, Sesame." As

Ali Baba climbed up a large, thick tree.

soon as the captain of the robbers had uttered these words, a door opened in the rock, and having made all his troop enter before him, he followed them, when the door closed of itself.

The robbers stayed some time within the rock, and Ali Baba, who feared that someone, or all of them together, might come out and catch him if

14

he should endeavour to make his escape, was obliged to sit patiently in the tree. At last the door opened again, and the forty thieves came out. As the captain went in last he came out first, and stood to see them all pass by him, when Ali Baba heard him make the door close by pronouncing these words "Shut, Sesame." Every man went and bridled his horse, fastened his wallet, and mounted again; and when the captain saw them all ready he put himself at their head, and they returned the way they had come.

Ali Baba did not immediately quit his tree, for, said he to himself, "They may have forgotten something, and may come back again, and then I shall be taken" He followed them with his eyes as far as he could see them, and after a considerable time descended, and had the curiosity to try if he could open the door by pronouncing the same words as the captain.

Making his way through the shrubs, he perceived the door concealed behind them, stood before it and said · "Open, Sesame." The door instantly flew wide open. Ali Baba, who expected a dark, dismal cavern, was surprised to see it well lighted and spacious, in the form of a vault, which received the light from an opening at the top of the rock. He saw all sorts of provisions, rich bales of silk, stuff, brocade, and valuable carpeting, piled upon one another, gold and silver ingots in great heaps, and money in bags. The sight of all these riches made him suppose that this cave must have been occupied for ages by robbers, who had succeeded one another.

Ali Baba did not stand long enough to consider what he should do, but went immediately into the cave, and as soon as he had entered the door shut of itself. But this did not disturb him, because he knew the secret to open it again. He did not trouble about the silver, but made the best use of his time in carrying out as much of the gold coin, which was in bags, as he thought his three asses could carry. He loaded the asses with the bags and laid the wood over them in such a manner that they could not be seen. When he had finished he stood before the door, and, pronouncing the words "Shut, Sesame," the door closed after him, for though it had shut itself when he was within the cave, it remained open while he was out. He then made the best of his way to town. When he reached home, he drove his asses into a little yard, shut the gates very carefully, threw off the wood that covered the bags, carried them into his house, and ranged them in order before his wife. She handled the bags, and, finding them full of money, suspected that her husband had been robbing, insomuch that she could not help saying, "Ali Baba, have you been so unhappy as to——" "Be quiet, wife," interrupted

14*

Ali Baba, "do not frighten yourself, I am no robber, unless he may be one who steals from robbers" He then emptied the bags of gold into a dazzling heap and told his wife the whole adventure from beginning to end, and, above all, recommended her to keep it secret

The wife rejoiced with her husband at their good fortune, and was anxious to count the money piece by piece, but from this Ali Baba dissuaded her

"If you begin to count you will never have done," said he; "I will dig a hole and bury it: there is no time to be lost."

"But at least, husband," said she, "let us know as near as possible how much we have. I will borrow a small measure in the neighbourhood and measure it, while you dig the hole."

Ali Baba was somewhat opposed, even to this, but his wife had so set her mind on knowing how much gold they possessed, that she ran to the house of her brother-in-law Cassim, who lived close by, and begged his wife to lend her a measure for a little while. The sister-in-law readily agreed, but as she knew Ali Baba's poverty, she was curious to know what sort of grain his wife wanted to measure, and artfully put some sticky substance at the bottom of the measure before giving it to her sister-in-law.

Ali Baba's wife went home, set the measure

upon the heap of gold, filled it and emptied it again and again until she knew the exact quantity they possessed. Ali Baba then buried the gold, and his wife carried the measure back to their sister-in-law, but without noticing that a piece of gold had stuck to the bottom, thanked her for the loan of it, and returned home.

As soon as Ali Baba's wife was gone Cassim's wife looked at the bottom of the measure and was very much surprised to find a piece of gold stuck to it. Envy immediately possessed her breast, for she could not bear to think that Ali Baba had so much gold that he had to measure and not count it She waited impatiently for her husband's return from his counting house, for she was anxious to acquaint him with what she had discovered.

"Cassim," said she, when at length he returned, "I know you think yourself rich, but you are mistaken if you think your brother Ali Baba is less well off than you. He does not count his money, —he has so much that he measures it."

Cassim asked her to explain, which she did, and also showed him the piece of money she had found.

Instead of being pleased at his brother's good fortune, Cassim was very jealous. After having married a rich widow he had never treated Ali Baba as a brother, being too proud to notice him as such, and so he went to him the next morning and said angrily "How is it that you pretend to be so poor and yet need a measure to measure your gold?"

"How, brother?" replied Ali Baba, "I do not know what you mean; explain yourself!"

"Do not pretend ignorance," replied Cassim, showing him the piece of gold his wife had given him "My wife found this at the bottom of the measure you borrowed yesterday."

Ali Baba at once perceived that, by his wife's folly, Cassim and his wife knew all they wished to conceal, and so, without showing the least surprise or trouble, he told his brother by what chance he had discovered the retreat of the thieves and where the place was situated. He offered him part of his treasure to keep the secret.

Cassim, after threatening to give information against Ali Baba unless he were told absolutely everything, including the magic words which opened the door of the cave, went away well satisfied He did not intend to share with his brother, but meant to be beforehand with him, hoping to get all the treasure to himself. He rose the next morning, long before the sun, and set out for the forest with ten mules bearing great chests, and followed the road which Ali Baba had described to him. Before long he reached the rock, found the entrance to the cavern, and pronounced the words, "Open,

Sesame " The door immediately opened, and when he was in, closed upon him. In examining the cave he was delighted to find even more treasure than Ali Baba had told him of. He could have feasted his eyes all day upon the wealth he saw, but remembered that the robbers might be returning and that he had no time to lose. He carried a great number of bags of gold to the door of the cavern, but on no account could he think of the necessary word to make it open. He tried and tried again, but the more he endeavoured to remember the word the more confused his memory became. He walked distractedly up and down the cavern, caring nothing for the wealth around him, but only longing to regain his liberty.

About noon the robbers chanced to visit their cave, and at some distance from it saw Cassim's mules straggling about the rock, with great chests on their backs Alarmed at this novelty, they galloped full speed to the cave. They drove away the mules, which Cassim had neglected to fasten, and they had soon strayed far out of sight in the forest. The robbers never gave themselves the trouble to pursue them, being more concerned to know whom they belonged to. While some of them searched about the rock, the captain and the rest went directly to the door, with their naked sabres in their hands, and, uttering the words "Open, Sesame," it opened

Cassim, who heard the noise of the horses' feet, never doubted of the arrival of the robbers, and his approaching death, but was resolved to make an effort to escape from them. To this end he rushed to the door, and no sooner saw it open than he ran out and threw the leader down, but could not escape the other robbers, who with their sabres soon deprived him of life.

After this the robbers' first care was to examine the cave. They found all the bags of gold which Cassim had brought to the door and carried them again to their places, without missing what Ali Baba had taken away before. Then, holding a council, they deliberated as to what course they should pursue to protect their cave in future.

They could not imagine how Cassim had entered it; they could not believe he had come in by the door, because it was evident by his being caught in the cave that he had not been able to make the door open to let him out they therefore supposed he did not know the secret As it was a matter of great importance to them to secure their riches, they agreed to cut Cassim's body in four pieces, to hang two on one side and two on the other, just within the door of the cave, to terrify any person who should attempt to enter it.

Having put their resolution into execution, they left the cave, mounted their horses and departed.

When night fell and Cassim did not return
his wife became very uneasy. She ran to Ali Baba
in alarm and said, "I believe, brother-in-law, you
know Cassim, your brother, is gone to the forest,
and upon what account; it is now night and he
is not returned; I am afraid some misfortune has
happened to him"

Ali Baba, who had guessed that his brother had
gone to the forest, made no reflection on his un-
generous conduct in thus seeking to take advantage
of him, but told his sister-in-law she need not
frighten herself, for that certainly Cassim would not
think it proper to come into the town till the night
should be pretty far advanced.

Cassim's wife, considering how much it concerned her husband to keep the business secret,
was the more easily persuaded to believe her
brother-in-law She went home again and waited
patiently until midnight. Then her fears redoubled,
and her grief was the greater in that she was
forced to keep it to herself. She repented of her
foolish curiosity, and wished she had never tried
to penetrate into the affairs of her brother- and
sister-in-law.

She spent all the night in weeping, and as
soon as it was day went to them, telling them,
with tears, the cause of her coming.

Ali Baba did not wait for his sister-in-law to
desire him to go and see what had become of

Cassim, but departed immediately with his three asses, begging of her first to moderate her affliction. He went to the forest, and when he came near the rock, having met neither his brother nor the mules by the way, was seriously alarmed at finding some blood spilt near the door, which he looked upon as an ill omen; but when he had pronounced the magic words, and the door had opened, he was struck with horror at the dismal sight that met his gaze.

He cut down the ghastly remains of his brother's body, placing them upon one ass, whilst the other two asses he loaded with bags of gold He placed wood above them and above his brother's body, so that no one could detect what he was carrying, and then drove the asses to the edge of the forest, where he waited until nightfall before venturing into the town.

When he reached home, he drove the two asses laden with gold into his little yard, and left the care of unloading them to his wife, while he led the other to his sister-in-law's house. Ali Baba knocked at the door, which was opened by Morgiana, an intelligent slave girl. When he came into the court, he unloaded the ass, and, taking Morgiana aside, said to her· "The first thing I ask of you is an inviolable secrecy, which you will find is necessary both for your mistress' sake and mine. Your master's body is contained in these bundles,

and our business is to bury him as if he had
died a natural death. Go, tell your mistress I
want to speak with her, and mind what I have
said to you."

Morgiana went to her mistress and soon brought
Ali Baba into her presence.

"Brother," said she with great impatience, "what
news do you bring me of my
husband?"

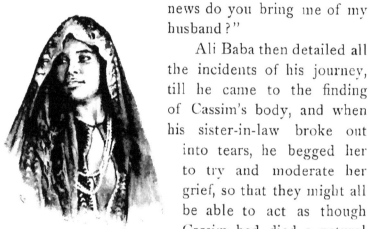

Ali Baba then detailed all
the incidents of his journey,
till he came to the finding
of Cassim's body, and when
his sister-in-law broke out
into tears, he begged her
to try and moderate her
grief, so that they might all
be able to act as though
Cassim had died a natural
death.

Morgiana.

Cassim's widow agreed to act her part, and Ali
Baba next took Morgiana into his confidence and
instructed her how to act her part well; he then
returned home with the ass.

Morgiana went out at the same time to an
apothecary, and asked for a particular kind of lozenges,
which he prepared, and which were very efficacious
in the most dangerous disorders. The apothecary
enquired who was ill at her master's. She replied,

with a sigh, it was her good master Cassim himself, that they knew not what his disorder was, but that he could neither eat nor speak. After these words Morgiana carried the lozenges home with her, and the next morning went to the same apothecary again, and, with tears in her eyes, asked for an essence which they used to give to sick people only when at the last extremity. "Alas!" said she, taking it from the apothecary, "I am afraid that this remedy will have no better effect than the lozenges, and that I shall lose my good master."

As Ali Baba and his wife were seen to go to and fro between Cassim's house and their own all that day, and appeared very melancholy, nobody was surprised in the evening to hear the lamentable shrieks and cries of Cassim's wife and Morgiana, who gave out everywhere that Cassim was dead.

The next morning, soon after day appeared, Morgiana, who knew a certain old cobbler who opened his stall earlier than most people, went to him and, bidding him good morning, put a piece of gold into his hand. "Well," said Baba Mustapha, which was his name, and who was a merry old fellow, "this is good handling, and no mistake What must I do for it? I am ready."

"Baba Mustapha," said Morgiana, "you must take with you your sewing tackle, and go with me; but when we come to a certain place I shall blindfold you."

Baba Mustapha seemed to hesitate a little at
these words. "Oh! oh!" replied he, "you would
have me do something against my conscience or
against my honour?"

"Nay," said Morgiana, putting another piece of
gold into his hand, "what I ask of you is nothing

"*You would have me do something against my conscience?*"

contrary to your honour; only come along with me
and fear nothing."

Baba Mustapha went with Morgiana, who, after
she had bound his eyes with a handkerchief at the
place she had mentioned, conveyed him to her
deceased master's house, and never unloosed his
eyes till he had entered the room where she had

put the parts of her master's body "Baba Mustapha," said she, "you must make haste and sew these quarters together, and when you have done I will give you another piece of gold"

After Baba Mustapha had finished his task, she blindfolded him again, gave him the third piece of gold as she had promised, and, recommending secrecy to him, led him back to the place where she first bound his eyes, pulled off the bandage, and let him go home, but watched him to see that he returned to his stall, for fear he should have the curiosity to return and follow her, when she knew all was safe she went home.

By the time Morgiana reached home Ali Baba was there and every preparation for the burying of the deceased man was made. The neighbours arrived and Cassim's body was carried to the burying ground, followed by the ministers of the mosque; Morgiana came next, beating her breast and tearing her hair, and Ali Baba followed after with all their friends and relations. Cassim's wife stayed at home mourning and uttering lamentable cries with the women of the neighbourhood, according to the custom.

In this way the manner of Cassim's death was hushed up between Cassim's widow, Ali Baba and his wife, and Morgiana, and nobody in the city had the least knowledge or suspicion.

Soon afterwards, deeming it more prudent that

they should all live together, Ali Baba and his wife went to live in Cassim's house. Their household goods were openly taken to the widow's house, but the gold that had been taken from the robbers' cave was conveyed thither by night.

But to return to the forty thieves. When they next visited their retreat in the forest they were greatly surprised to find Cassim's body taken away and some of their bags of gold missing.

"Without doubt," said the captain, "the man we discovered here had an accomplice, and unless we succeed in catching him we shall gradually lose all the riches which our ancestors and ourselves have amassed with so much pains and danger.

"I propose, therefore, that one of you should go into the town, disguised as a traveller and a stranger, to try if he can hear any talk of the curious death of the man whom we killed, endeavour to find out where he lived and who he was. It may be a perilous undertaking to venture into the town where for so long we have been unknown, and remember, also, that should he who undertakes the commission be found betraying us in any way, he shall immediately suffer death at our hands."

The forty thieves agreed to all their captain proposed, and one of their number at once volunteered to undertake the commission

He disguised himself and, taking leave of the

troop at night, went into the town just at daybreak,
and walked up and down, till accidentally he came
to Baba Mustapha's stall, which was always open
before any of the shops

Baba Mustapha was seated with an awl in his
hand, just going to work. The robber saluted him,
bidding him good-morrow, and, seeing that he was
very old, said "Honest man, you begin to work
very early. How is it one of your age can see so
well? I should have doubted, even had it been
lighter, whether you could have seen to stitch."

"Certainly," replied Baba Mustapha, "you must
be a stranger, and do not know me: for, old as I
am, I have extraordinary good eyes, and you will
not doubt it when I tell you that I sewed a dead
body together in a place where I had not so much
light as I have now."

The robber was overjoyed to think that he had
addressed himself so soon to a man who in all probability could give him the intelligence he wanted.
"A dead body!" he replied with affected amazement, "what could you sew up a dead body for?
You mean you sewed up his winding sheet." "No,
no," answered Baba Mustapha, "I perceive I have
betrayed myself; you want me to speak out, but
you shall know no more."

The robber wanted no farther assurance to be
persuaded that he had discovered what he sought.
He pulled out a piece of gold and, putting it into

Baba Mustapha's hand, said to him, "I do not want to learn your secret, though I can assure you I would not divulge it if you trusted me with it. The only thing which I desire of you is, to do me the favour to show me the house where you stitched up the dead body."

"If I were disposed to do you that favour," replied Baba Mustapha, holding the money in his hand, "I assure you I cannot, and you may believe me on my word. I was taken to a certain place, where I was blindfolded, I was then led to the house, and afterwards brought back in the same manner."

"Well," replied the robber, "you may remember a little of the way. Come, let me blindfold your eyes and I will walk beside you And as everyone should be paid for his trouble, here is another piece of gold for you." And he put another piece of money into the old man's hand

The two pieces of gold were a great temptation; Baba Mustapha looked at them without saying a word, but at length he put them in his purse and consented to do as the robber wished

He first led the robber to the place where Morgiana had blindfolded him, and the robber tied his handkerchief over his eyes and then walked by his side, partly leading him and partly guided by him. "I think," said Baba Mustapha at length, "I went no farther," and he stopped directly at Cassim's house, where Ali Baba now lived. Before taking the handkerchief off the old man's eyes, the thief carefully marked the door with a piece of chalk, which he had ready in his hand, and then asked if he knew whose house that was · to which Baba Mustapha replied, that as he did not live in that neighbourhood he could not tell.

The robber, finding he could discover no more from the old man, thanked him for the trouble he had taken, and left him to go back to his stall, while he returned to the forest, persuaded that he would be very well received by his comrades.

A little while after the robber and Baba Mustapha had parted, Morgiana went out of the house upon some errand, and upon her return, seeing the mark the robber had made, stopped to observe it.

"What can be the meaning of this mark?" said she to herself; "somebody intends my new master no good. however, with whatever intention it was done, it is best to guard against the worst." Accordingly she fetched a piece of chalk and marked two or three doors on each side in the same manner, without saying a word to her master or mistress.

In the meantime the thief rejoined his troop in the forest and recounted his success to them, expatiating upon his good fortune in so soon meeting the

only person who could inform him of what he wanted to know.

All the thieves listened to him with the utmost satisfaction, and the captain, after commending his diligence, said: "Comrades, we have no time to

lose: let us set off well armed, without its appearing who we are; but that we may not excite any suspicion, let only one or two go into the town together, and join at our rendezvous, which shall be the great square. Our comrade, who brought us the good news, and I will go and find out the house, that we may consult what had best be done."

This plan being approved of by all, they were soon ready. They filed off in parties of two and succeeded in entering the town without being suspected.

Morgiana marked two or three doors in the same manner.

The robber who had played the part of spy in the morning led the captain into the street where Ali Baba was now living, and when they came to the first of the houses which Morgiana had marked, he pointed it out. But the captain observed that the next door was chalked in the same manner in the same place, and, showing it to his guide, asked him what it meant.

15*

The guide was so astounded he knew not what answer to make, and was still more puzzled when he and the captain saw five or six houses similarly marked. He declared he had marked but one, and could not tell who had chalked the rest, so that he was unable to distinguish the house the cobbler had stopped at.

The captain returned directly to the square which was to be the meeting place and ordered all the robbers to return to the forest. As soon as they arrived there the reason of their returning was explained to them, and the robber who had failed in what he had undertaken to do was immediately put to death.

Another of the troop, whom not even the fear of death, should he fail, could daunt, undertook to find out the house.

He presented himself to Baba Mustapha as the first robber had done, and, being shown the house, marked it with red chalk in a place which he thought not likely to be noticed.

Not long afterwards Morgiana, whose eyes nothing could escape, went out, and seeing the red chalk marked the neighbours' houses in the same manner, by way of precaution.

The robber returned to his comrades and recounted what he had done, and the captain and all of them thought the plan must succeed.

They stole into the town with the same precaution as before, but on coming into the street they were again baffled by seeing the same marks on several doors. The captain was very angry, and when he and the rest of the troop had returned to the forest the robber who had been the cause of the mistake underwent the·same punishment as had been meted out to the first.

The captain, having lost two brave fellows of his troop, was afraid of diminishing it too much by pursuing this plan to get information of the residence of their plunderer.

He had found that his men's heads were not so good as their hands on such occasions, and therefore resolved to take upon himself the important commission.

Accordingly he went and addressed himself to Baba Mustapha, who did him the same service he had done to the other robbers. He did not set any particular mark on the house, but examined it so carefully that by passing it often it became impossible for him to mistake it.

Well satisfied with his attempt, the captain returned to the forest and joined his comrades in the cave, telling them that nothing could now prevent their taking revenge upon the man who had succeeded in gaining knowledge of their secret

He had made a plan, and in order to carry it out he sent them to the neighbouring villages to

buy nineteen mules and thirty-eight large leather
jars, one full of oil, the others empty.

In a few days' time the robbers had purchased
the mules and jars, and, after having put one of his
men into each, he rubbed the outside of the jars
with oil from the full vessel. .

The thieves had originally been forty in number,
thirty-nine men and the captain : there remained now
only thirty-seven men; the captain saw that the
nineteen mules were laden with his men in the
jars and the jar full of oil and set out with them
towards the town, reaching it in the dusk of the
evening, as he had intended.

He led the laden mules through the streets
until he came to Ali Baba's house, at whose door
he meant to knock; but seeing him seated in the
doorway, taking a little fresh air, he stopped his
mules, addressed himself to him, and said . "I have
brought some oil a great way, to sell at to-morrow's
market; and it is now so late that I do not know
where to lodge. If I should not be troublesome to
you, do me the favour to let me pass the night
with you, and I shall be very much obliged by your
hospitality."

Although Ali Baba had seen the captain of the
robbers in the forest, he did not recognise him in
the disguise of an oil merchant He made him welcome to his house and opened his gates for the
mules to go into the yard He called a slave, named

Abdoolah, and ordered him, when the mules were unladen, not only to put them into the stable, but to give them fodder; then he bade Morgiana get a good supper for his guest, and sat talking with him until he had eaten it.

It was not until Ali Baba had retired to rest that the captain found means of visiting the yard. He took the lid off each of the jars, to give his men a little air, and bade them be ready to come out as soon as he gave them the signal. After this he returned to the house, when Morgiana, taking up a light, conducted him to his chamber, where she left him; and he, to avoid any suspicion, put the light out soon after, and laid himself down in his clothes, that he might be the more ready to rise.

Morgiana, who had not yet finished her work, found to her mortification, when her lamp suddenly went out, that she had no more oil in the house; what to do she did not know, till the slave who had been called to stable the supposed merchant's mules advised her to take a little from the thirty-eight jars which stood in the courtyard.

So Morgiana took the oil-pot, and went into the yard; what was her surprise upon approaching the first jar when the robber within it said softly "Is it time?"

Many would have uttered an exclamation of alarm, but not so Morgiana. Comprehending at

once that some danger threatened her master, she
only replied in a whisper "Not yet, but presently."
She went in this manner to all the jars, hearing the
same question and giving the same answer, till she
came to the jar of oil.

By this means she found out that her master,
instead of entertaining a harmless oil merchant, had
admitted thirty-eight robbers to his house. She
made what haste she could to fill her oil-pot, and
returned to her kitchen, when, as soon as she had
lighted her lamp, she took a great kettle, went
again to the oil-jar, and filled the kettle with oil, set
it over a large fire, and as soon as it boiled went
out and poured sufficient of the boiling oil into each
jar to stifle the robber within it.

All this she accomplished without making any
noise, and having put out her lamp she waited to
hear what would happen.

Before long the captain of the robbers got up
and opened his window, gave the appointed signal,
which was to drop a few small stones from the
window, but growing uneasy that he received no
response, he went down into the yard. He went to
the first jar and spoke softly. There was no answer,
and then he noticed the smell of hot oil and soon
discovered what had happened.

Examining all the jars, one after another, he
found all his comrades were dead, and deemed it
best to make his escape whilst he yet might. He

found a door in the yard which opened into the garden, and climbing over the wall made his way back to the forest.

When Morgiana was satisfied that all danger for the present was over, and that she had saved her master and his family, she retired to bed and to sleep.

The captain found all his comrades were dead.

Ali Baba rose early and went to the bath. When he returned he was very much surprised to see the oil-jars and to find that the merchant had gone.

He enquired of Morgiana how this came about, and by way of answer she led him to the first jar and bade him look inside.

Ali Baba did so, and, seeing a man, started back in alarm, and cried out. "Do not be afraid," said Morgiana, "the man you see there can neither do you nor anybody else any harm. He is dead. Look into the other jars."

When he had done so he stood staring at Morgiana for some time in silence, and when at length he recovered himself sufficiently to be able to speak, he said· "And what has come of the merchant?"

"Merchant!" answered she, "he is as much one as I am." She then recounted to her master exactly all that had happened, telling him how she had suspected treachery from the time she had first observed the chalk marks upon the door

"If you reflect on all that has happened," said she, "you will find it was a plot of the robbers whom you saw in the forest. Thirty-seven have now perished, but the captain and two others are still unaccounted for. Therefore it behoves you to be upon your guard, and for my part I shall neglect nothing necessary for your preservation"

When Morgiana ceased speaking, Ali Baba was so sensible of the great service she had done him that he said to her: "I will not die without rewarding you as you deserve I owe my life to you, and for the first token of my acknowledgement I give you your liberty. You are no longer a slave. All we have now to do is to bury the bodies of these wicked thieves with all the secrecy imaginable, that

nobody may suspect what is become of them. But
that labour Abdoolah and I will undertake."

Ali Baba's garden was very long, and shaded
at the farther end by a great number of large trees.
Under these he and the slave dug a trench, long
and wide enough to hold all the robbers, and here

The robbers were all buried in Ali Baba's garden.

they were all buried. When this was done they
hid the jars and weapons, and as they had no use
for the mules, Ali Baba sent them, at different times,
to be sold in the market.

But the captain of the band of robbers was
not long before he planned revenge for the loss of

his brave comrades   He had no intention of remaining the sole occupant of the cave, but before
collecting a fresh troop he meant to put an end to
the man who was in possession of such a dangerous
secret.

So the morning after his comrades had been
destroyed he went into the town and took up his
lodging at an inn.   He asked the host what news
he had, and as the worthy man gave him all sorts
of information, but none of a kind that interested
him, he judged that Ali Baba had thought best to
keep the whole affair a secret

He now determined to play the part of a silk
merchant, and for this purpose engaged a warehouse
immediately opposite that which had belonged to
Cassim and which was now in charge of Ali Baba's
son.

He very soon made friends with the young man,
and, being well disguised, ventured also to get into
conversation with Ali Baba and was again invited to
spend an evening at his house.

Morgiana no sooner set eyes on him than she
mistrusted him, more especially so when he declared
that he had a special aversion to salt and begged
that none might be used in preparing the evening
meal.

Everyone knows that amongst Eastern nations
if a man has once eaten salt with his enemy he
will not harm him, and wise Morgiana was quite

Morgiana held a dagger in her hand.

certain that this was the reason the pretended silk merchant would not eat salt at her master's table. When she perceived, moreover, that he had a dagger hidden beneath his garments she determined to put an end to him herself. And so, when supper was over, she came in to dance before her master and his guest. The dance was a strange one, for she held a dagger in her hand and as she twirled about she made a pretence of presenting it now at her master's breast, now at his son's, and finally plunged it into the robber's heart.

Ali Baba and his son were shocked at this action, until Morgiana opened the pretended merchant's garment and showed them the dagger. "Look well at him," she said, tearing the false beard from his face, "and you will find him to be both the fictitious oil-merchant and the captain of the forty thieves"

Ali Baba and his son knew not how to express their gratitude to the brave Morgiana

"I gave you your liberty," said Ali Baba, "and promised that my gratitude should not cease there, but I now intend giving you a higher proof of my esteem by making you my daughter-in-law." Then, turning to his son, he said· "Consider that by marrying Morgiana you marry the preserver of our family."

As the son readily consented to the marriage the nuptials were celebrated a few days later.

The captain's body was buried in the same trench as the rest of the troop and no one was ever any the wiser concerning the matter.

Ali Baba waited for a whole year after his son's marriage before venturing near the cave, because the end of the two robbers whom the crosses had caused to be put to death was still unknown to him.

However, at length he decided to venture to return to the cave. Finding that it had evidently been undisturbed since the captain's death he decided that the troop of forty robbers was now completely destroyed. He took away with him as much gold as he could carry, and afterwards took his son to the cave and taught him the secret, which they handed down to their posterity, who, using their good fortune with moderation, lived always in great honour and splendour.

THE
STORY OF KUMMIR AL ZUMMAUN
AND BADOURA, PRINCESS OF CHINA.

Badoura, Princess of China.

ABOUT twenty days' sail from the coast of Persia, there are islands in the main ocean called the Islands of the Children of Khaledan. These islands were formerly governed by a king named Shaw Zummaun, who would have thought himself one of the most happy monarchs in the world, on account of his peaceful and prosperous reign, had it not been that he had been denied the blessing of children. He had no son to succeed him on the throne, and this caused him great grief and uneasiness.

Think then of his joy when, in his old age, Heaven sent him a son, and the prince was so beautiful that he gave him the name of Kummir al Zummaun, which means "Moon of the Age."

He was brought up with all imaginable care, and when he had arrived at a proper age, his father appointed him an experienced governor and able preceptors. He learned all he was taught and acquitted himself with such grace and wonderful address, as to charm all who saw him, and particularly the sultan his father

When he had grown to early manhood, his father, now being advanced in age, began to think of retirement, and wished to resign the throne to the prince. "I have borne the fatigue of a crown till I am weary of it," said he, "and think it is now proper for me to retire"

He then informed the prince that he wished him to make a suitable marriage before he was publicly announced king.

But the prince had no wish to marry, and said so very plainly.

The prince's father was not a little grieved to discover his aversion to marriage, yet would not charge him with disobedience, nor exert his paternal authority. He contented himself with telling him he would not force his inclinations, but give him time to consider the proposal.

However, when at the end of another year the prince still declared his intention of remaining single, the king was very much annoyed. He took council with his vizier, who counselled him to have patience.

"Patience," said he, "brings many things about that before seemed impracticable. Your Majesty will have no cause to reproach yourself for precipitation, if you will give the prince another year to consider your proposal."

The sultan, who so anxiously desired to see his son married, thought this long delay an age; however, though with much difficulty, he yielded to his grand vizier's advice.

But the year expired, and, to the great regret of the sultan, Prince Kummir al Zummaun gave not the least proof of having changed his sentiments.

One day, therefore, when there was a great Council, the sultan addressed him thus, in the hearing of all his Court. "My son, it is now a long while since I expressed to you my earnest desire to see you married, and I imagined you would have had more regard for my wishes, but after such a resistance on your part I have thought fit to propose the same to you in the presence of my Council."

The prince answered with so much warmth that he would not comply with his father's request, that the sultan, enraged to see himself thwarted by him in full Council, ordered the guards to take the prince away, and carry him to an old tower that had long been unoccupied, where he was shut up, with only a bed, a little furniture, some books, and one slave to attend him.

Kummir al Zummaun, thus deprived of liberty, was nevertheless pleased to be alone with his books, which made him regard his confinement with indifference. In the evening he bathed and said his prayers, and after having read some chapters in the Koran, with the same tranquillity of mind as if he had been in the sultan's palace, he undressed himself and went to bed, leaving his lamp burning by him while he slept.

In this tower was a well, which served in the daytime for a retreat to a certain fairy called Maimorme. It was about midnight when Maimorme sprang lightly to the mouth of the well, to wander about the world after her wonted custom, where her curiosity led her. She was surprised to see a light in the prince's chamber, and, entering, approached the bedside

The prince was fast asleep; but notwithstanding that his eyes were veiled the fairy thought him the finest young man she had ever seen. She kissed him gently, without waking him, and took her flight into the air. As she was ascending she heard a great flapping of wings, and knew it to be a genie who made the noise. This genie's name was Danhasch, and Maimorme at once accosted him and asked him where he came from, what he had seen, and what he had done that night.

"Since you desire to know," replied Danhasch, "I will inform you that I come from the utmost

limits of China; the king of that country has an
only daughter, the finest woman that ever was seen
in the world. Her hair is brown, and of such length
as to trail on the ground, her forehead is as smooth
as the best polished mirror, her eyes are black,

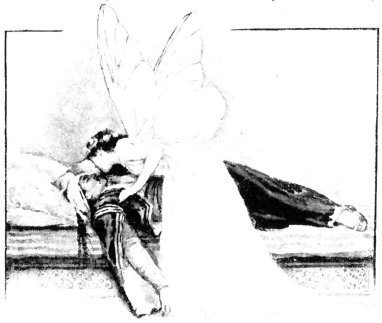

Maimoune kissed him gently, without waking him.

sparkling, and full of fire, her nose is neither too
long nor too short, and her mouth small and of a
vermilion colour. Her teeth are like two rows of
pearls, and surpass the finest in whiteness. In a
word, by this imperfect sketch, you may guess there
is no beauty likely to exceed her in the world.

"Her father loves her beyond all belief and has built for her seven palaces, the most extraordinary and magnificent that ever were known, and has furnished them most sumptuously.

"Because of the fame of this incomparable princess's beauty, the most powerful neighbouring kings have sent ambassadors to solicit her in marriage. The King of China received them all in the same obliging manner, but as he resolved not to marry his daughter without her consent, and she did not like any of the parties, the ambassadors were forced to return as they came.

"'Sir,' said the princess to the king her father, 'you have an inclination to see me married, and think to oblige me by it, but where shall I find such stately palaces and delicious gardens as are furnished me by your Majesty? Through your good pleasure I am under no constraint and have the same honours shown to me as are paid to yourself These are advantages I cannot expect to find anywhere else, whoever may be my husband; men love to be masters, and I have no inclination to be commanded.'

"The king bore with her whim for some time; but when a very powerful and more opulent king asked her hand in marriage and she treated him with the same scorn she had shown towards the others, he became enraged and shut her up in a single apartment, with only ten old women to wait

upon her and keep her company, the chief of whom
had been her nurse."

Maimorme, having listened to the story of the
Princess of China, told her story of the Prince
Kummir al Zummaun, and as both the genie and
the fairy persisted in saying that their special charge
was more beautiful than the other, Danhasch agreed

Danhasch returned, bringing the fair princess with him asleep.

to go and fetch the princess that they might compare
the two.

Accordingly Danhasch flew off towards China,
whence he soon returned with incredible speed,
bringing the fair princess with him asleep. He set
her down by the prince's bedside, and truly it was
difficult to determine which was the more beautiful
of the two. Neither Maimorme nor Danhasch would
yield, and it was not until Maimorme had summoned

a hideous humpbacked genie, named Caochcash, that the matter was decided, and he declared that the prince and princess were both equally beautiful. It was he, too, who suggested that they should awaken the two sleepers in turn, and see what they thought of one another.

So Maimorme transformed herself into a flea and bit the prince. No sooner was he awake than he espied the sleeping princess and straightway fell in love with her. He kissed her tenderly, but she did not awaken, because she was sleeping an enchanted sleep. He next drew a ring from the princess's finger and replaced it with one from his own; after this he again fell into a profound and enchanted sleep.

Danhasch next transformed himself into a flea and in his turn bit the princess, who awoke from her sleep, and on opening her eyes was very much surprised to see a handsome young prince lying by her side, fast asleep.

She fell in love with him at once, as he had done with her, and was somewhat disappointed that she could not awaken him. She kissed his cheek and shook him several times; but all in vain, and very soon she too fell asleep.

Then Maimorme bade Danhasch carry her back to her own apartment, this he did, and as day began to appear Maimorme retired to her well.

Kummir al Zummaun, on waking next morning,

Kummir al Zummaun awakened his slave.

at once looked for the lady he had seen during the night, but she had vanished.

He awakened his slave, who was still asleep, and asked him what had become of the lady who had visited him during the night.

"My Lord," answered the slave, "I know not what lady your Highness speaks of."

The prince flew into a violent rage, and as the slave persisted in saying that no lady had been there, his master beat him soundly and, fastening a rope under his arms, plunged him into the well and threatened to drown him unless he at once confessed the truth.

The slave, perplexed and half dead, said within himself, "The prince must have lost his senses through grief, and I shall not escape if I do not tell him a falsehood. My Lord," he cried, in a suppliant tone, "I beseech your Highness to spare my life, and I will tell you the truth."

The prince drew the slave up, but as soon as he was out of the well he begged leave to go and change his wet clothes before he told the story. Having obtained permission he went out, and having locked the door upon the prince, ran to the palace just as he was, and informed the king that the prince had taken leave of his senses and raved continually of a lady whom he had seen during the night; he also called the king's attention to the violence with which he had been treated.

The king and his vizier went immediately to examine into the condition of the prince, and after hearing his story the king could no longer believe that his son had lost his senses, strange though the circumstances appeared to be. The prince showed his father the ring upon his finger, which he had taken from that of the sleeping princess, and begged his father to delay no longer, but to unite him to the lady with whom he had fallen so deeply in love.

"Alas, my son," replied the king, "I would I knew who she is. I would instantly comply with your wishes, and should be the happiest father in the world! But where shall I seek her? How came she here, and by what conveyance, without my consent? These things I confess I do not understand." As he spoke he took the prince by the hand, and said, "Come then, my son, let us go and grieve together; you with hopeless love, and I with seeing your affliction, without being able to afford you relief."

Shaw Zummaun then led his son out of the tower, and conveyed him to the palace, where he had no sooner arrived than, in despair at loving an unknown object, he fell sick, and took to his bed, the king shut himself up with him, without attending to the affairs of his kingdom, for many days.

Whilst matters passed thus in the capital of Shaw Zummaun, things were no better with the Princess Badoura, by which name the Princess of China was called.

When she awoke next morning she immediately asked her women what had become of the handsome young man she had seen during the night. No one would believe her story, and her nurse and women slaves sought to convince her that it was quite impossible that any young man could have visited her, as she was locked into her room and they had all been sleeping by the door.

She became so angry that the nurse fetched the King and Queen of China, who visited their daughter and sought to convince her of her error. But when they could not do this, they became exceedingly concerned at the state of her mind.

The slave ran to the palace.

The king, being convinced that she was insane, ordered her to be more closely confined than ever, and allowed only the nurse to attend on her, with a good guard at the door of her apartment.

So anxious was he to effect her cure that he summoned his Council, and after having acquainted them with the princess's condition said: "If any of you is capable of restoring her to health, I will give her to him in marriage, and make him heir to my dominions."

The desire of obtaining a handsome young princess, and the hopes of one day governing so great a kingdom as that of China, had a great effect on an emir, already advanced in years, who was present at this Council. As he was well skilled in magic, he offered the king to recover his daughter, and flattered himself with success.

"I consent to the trial," said the king; "but I forgot to tell you one condition, and that is, that if you do not succeed, you shall lose your head. It would not be reasonable you should have so great a reward, and yet run no risk : and what I say to you," continued the king, "I say to all others who come after you, that they may consider beforehand what they undertake."

The emir accepted the condition, and the king conducted him to the princess's place of confinement.

But his magic arts availed him little . the princess continued to entreat her father to marry her to the handsome young prince, and at length the emir threw himself at his Majesty's feet and owned he had no power to cure her malady.

The king, enraged at his incapacity, and the trouble he had given him, caused him to be immediately beheaded

Some days after, unwilling to have it said that he had neglected his daughter's cure, the king put forth a proclamation in his capital, stating that if there were any physician, astrologer, or magician who would undertake to restore the princess to her senses, he should win her in marriage if he succeeded, or lose his head if he failed.

No less than a hundred and fifty astrologers, physicians, and magicians attempted to cure the princess of her malady, and all underwent the same fate, and their heads were set upon poles on every gate of the city

Now the Princess Badoura's nurse had a son whose name was Marzavan, who had been foster brother to the princess and brought up with her. Marzavan had travelled a great deal in foreign parts and was much skilled in astrology, geomancy and the like secret arts.

As soon as his mother heard he had returned from his travels she made up her mind to introduce him into the princess's presence that he might try his skill in curing her; but as she did not wish him to lose his head she disguised him as a woman and addressed herself to the chamberlain of the guard thus· "I have a daughter whom I brought up along with the princess; she has been since married, yet the princess still does her the honour to love her, and wishes to see her, without being observed."

The chamberlain interrupted her, and exclaimed, "Say no more, I will with pleasure do anything to oblige the princess; go and fetch your daughter, or send for her about midnight, and the gate shall be open for you."

As soon as it was dark the nurse went and fetched Marzavan, and so well was he disguised that the chamberlain never suspected him of being a man, but admitted him at once.

The nurse, however, took the precaution of telling the princess that the disguised woman was Marzavan, her foster brother.

"What! my brother Marzavan," exclaimed the princess, with great joy, "approach and take off that veil; for it is not unreasonable that a brother and sister should see each other without covering their faces. I rejoice to see you returned in good health, after so many years' absence."

"Madam," replied Marzavan, "I am infinitely obliged to you. I hoped to have heard a better account of your health than has been given me. It will, however, give me pleasure to help to remedy your Highness's situation.'

Having thus spoken he drew out a book and some other things which he thought he would require to aid him. The princess, observing these preparations, exclaimed, "What! brother, are you one of those who believe me mad? Undeceive yourself and hear me."

The princess then related to Marzavan all the particulars of the story, and showed him the ring which had been exchanged for hers.

After the princess had concluded Marzavan, filled with wonder and astonishment, remained for some time with his eyes fixed on the ground without speaking a word; but at length he lifted up his head and said "If it be as your Highness says, and I do not in the least doubt it, I do not despair of being able to procure you the gratification of your wishes. But I must first entreat your Highness to arm yourself with patience. I will at once set out in search of this prince, and when you hear of my return be assured I shall have found him."

Having thus spoken, he took leave of the princess, and set out the next morning on his intended travels.

He journeyed from city to city, from province to province, and from island to island, until after four months he arrived at Torf, a seaport town, where he found the talk was all of Prince Kummir al Zummaun, who was sick and whose history greatly resembled that of the Princess Badoura. Marzavan was extremely delighted, and at once informed himself where the prince was to be found and lost no time in arriving at Shaw Zummaun's capital

He obtained an audience of the grand vizier and informed him that, hearing of the young prince's malady, he wished to try and effect a cure, but first he must be told all the details concerning it.

The grand vizier then related the story of Prince Kummir al Zummaun from the time of his birth to

17

the date of his refusing to take a wife and the subsequent imprisonment in the tower and all that he
asserted had befallen him there. Marzavan gave
great attention to all the grand vizier said, and saw
no reason to doubt that the prince was the man
whom the Princess of China so ardently loved. Without explaining himself farther he desired to see the
prince, that he might be better able to judge of his
disorder and its cure.

"Follow me," said the grand vizier, and at once
led him into a room, where the prince was lying
upon a bed, languishing and with his eyes shut. Notwithstanding his condition, and regardless of the
presence of the king, his father, who was sitting by
him, he could not avoid exclaiming: "Was there
ever a greater resemblance?" For he noticed at
once that Prince Kummir al Zummaun and Princess
Badoura of China were exactly alike.

This exclamation of Marzavan's excited the
prince's curiosity and he opened his eyes. At once
Marzavan commenced to recite in verse all that had
happened between him and the Princess of China.
From this the prince had no reason to doubt but
that Marzavan knew her and could give him tidings
of her His countenance immediately brightened up
with joy, and Marzavan took the liberty of requesting
the king to allow him to take his place by his son's
side and to be left alone with him.

The king, overjoyed at the alteration in his

son's countenance, hastened to comply, and Marzavan was left alone with the prince Leaning down to him he said, "Prince, it is time you should cease to grieve The lady for whom you suffer is the Princess Badoura, daughter of the King of China. This I can assure your Highness from what she has told me of her adventure, and what I have learned of yours. She has suffered no less on your account than you have on hers." Here he related all that he knew of the princess's story, from the night of their extraordinary interview.

This account had a marvellous effect on the prince. He felt he had strength sufficient to rise, and at once began to dress himself. From that time his health began steadily to improve, and when he found himself in a condition to undertake the voyage he took Marzavan aside and said, "Dear Marzavan, it is now time to perform the promise you have made me. One thing still afflicts me, however, and that is the difficulty I shall find to obtain my father's permission to travel into a distant country. You observe he scarcely allows me to be a moment out of his sight."

Marzavan, in his anxiety to cure his beloved Princess Badoura, lost sight of the trouble he was about to cause the good Shaw Zummaun. "I have thought of a plan," said he. "You have not stirred abroad for some time, therefore request the king's permission to go upon a hunting party. He will no

17*

doubt comply. When you have obtained his leave, order two fleet coursers for each of us to be got ready, one to mount, the other to change, and leave the rest to me."

The following day the prince did as Marzavan had instructed him. The king gave his consent, and ordered the best horses in the royal stable for his use.

Kummin al Zummaun and Marzavan hunted, in company with the two grooms who led the spare horses, all the first day, and at night they alighted at a caravanserai, or inn, where they supped, and slept till about midnight, when Marzavan awakened the prince and desired him to change into another dress he had brought in his baggage for him. When he had done this, they stole softly out of the inn, leading the two spare horses, and having torn the prince's suit and dipped it in blood, they threw it by the roadside so that it might appear that the prince had been devoured by wild animals.

"The king will conclude I have escaped," said Marzavan, "that I was afraid to face his anger, having allowed you to come to harm."

The prince comforted himself with the reflection that if he were giving his father cause for great grief his joy would be the greater when he afterwards heard he was alive and well.

The prince and Marzavan, being well provided for their expenses, continued their journey both by

land and sea, and found no other obstacle but the
length of time which it necessarily took up. They
arrived at length at the capital of China, where
Marzavan, instead of going to his house, carried the
prince to a public inn. They remained there, in-
cognito, three days, to rest themselves after the
fatigue of the voyage, during which time Marzavan
caused an astrologer's habit to be made for the
prince. The three days being expired, they went
together to the bath, where the prince put on his
astrologer's dress from thence Marzavan conducted
him to the King of China's palace and there left
him.

As soon as he was alone the prince lifted up
his voice and cried "I am an astrologer and am
come to cure the illustrious Princess Badoura,
daughter of the most high and mighty King of
China, on the conditions proposed by his Majesty,
to marry her if I succeed, or else to lose my life
for my fruitless and presumptuous attempt."

It was some time since anyone had appeared
on this account, the ill-luck of the hundred and
fifty who had gone before being sufficient to deter
others

The prince's appearance, his noble air and
blooming youth, made everyone who saw him pity
him, and some tried to persuade him to abandon the
rash attempt and depart.

But the prince continued firm, until the grand

vizier came and introduced him into the presence
of the King of China, who also was moved to pity
by the sight of the prince's youth and comeliness,
and gave him an opportunity of withdrawing from
the attempt.

But the prince was so confident of success that
the king ordered him to be conducted into the princess's apartment.

The chief of the guards led him into a great
hall, which was divided from the princess's apartment
by a tapestry curtain   Here the prince stopped and
said. "It will be best to cure the princess without
seeing her, that you may be witness of my skill;
notwithstanding my impatience to see a princess of
her rank, who is to be my wife, yet out of respect
to you, I will deprive myself of that pleasure for a
little while." Being furnished with everything proper
for an astrologer to carry about him, he took pen,
ink, and paper out of his pocket, and wrote a little
note to the princess, explaining who he was, how
he had fallen in love with her upon the night he
had first seen her, and how he had changed his ring
for hers. He concluded by saying. "If you will
condescend to return his love, he will esteem himself
the happiest of mankind. If not, the sentence of
death, which your refusal must draw upon him, will
be received with resignation, since he will perish on
account of his love for you."

When the prince had finished his billet he

folded it up, and enclosed in it the princess's ring
"There, friend," said he to the guard, "carry this to
your mistress. If it does not cure her as soon as
she reads it and sees what it contains, I give you
leave to tell everybody that I am the most ignorant
and impudent astrologer that ever existed "

The guard, entering the princess's apartment, gave
her the packet. She opened the billet with indifference, but, when she saw the ring, she had not patience
to read it through, but rose and ran to the entrance
hall, where she saw and recognised the prince. They
embraced tenderly, without being able to speak for
excess of joy.

The princess's nurse made them come into the
apartment, where the Princess Badoura gave the
prince her ring, saying. "Take it, I cannot keep
it without restoring yours, which I will never part
with."

The guard went immediately to inform the king
what had happened· "Sir," said he, "all the astrologers and doctors who have hitherto pretended to
cure the princess were foolish and ignorant compared with the present. He cured her without
seeing her."

The king at once went to his daughter's apartment and embraced both her and the prince, and
taking his hand joined it to the princess's, saying
"Happy stranger, whoever you are, I will keep my
word and give you my daughter for your wife, though

by what I see in you, it is impossible for me to believe you are really what you pretend."

Kummir al Zummaun thanked the king. "As
for my condition," said he, "I must own I am not
an astrologer, as your Majesty has guessed; I only
put on the habit of one that I might succeed in
meeting the princess again." He then related his
history, and how wonderful had been the origin of
his love, that the princess's was altogether as marvellous, and that both were confirmed by the exchange of the two rings

The marriage was solemnized the same day, and
the rejoicings were universal all over the empire of
China. Nor was Marzavan forgotten. The king gave
him an honourable post in his Court, and a promise
of further advancement.

The feasting and rejoicing were kept up for
several months, but in the midst of them Kummir
al Zummaun dreamt one night that he saw his
father on his bed at the point of death, and heard
him thus address his attendants: "My son, whom I
so tenderly loved, has abandoned me and is the
cause of my death"

The prince awoke with a sigh and acquainted
the princess with the cause of his uneasiness. The
princess, who strove to please her husband in everything, went to her father the next day, kissed his
hand, and thus addressed him · "I have a favour to
beg of your Majesty, and I beseech you not to deny

me, but that you may not believe I ask it at the
solicitation of the prince my husband, I assure you
beforehand he knows nothing of my request. It is,
that you will grant me your permission to go with
him and visit his father."

"Daughter," replied the king, "though I shall
be sorry to part with you for so long a time as a
journey to a place so distant will require, yet I
cannot disapprove of your resolution—it is worthy of
yourself. go, child, I give you leave, but on
condition that you stay no longer than a year in
Shaw Zummaun's Court. I hope the king will agree
to this, that we shall alternately see, he his son and
his daughter-in-law, and I my daughter and my son-
in-law."

The princess communicated the King of China's
consent to her husband, who was transported to
receive it, and returned his thanks for this new
token of her love.

The King of China gave orders for preparations
to be made for their departure, and when all things
were ready, he accompanied the prince and princess
several days' journey on their way, when he took
leave of them with many tokens of endearment.

After travelling about a month, they one day
entered a plain of great extent, planted at convenient
distances with tall trees, forming an agreeable shade.
The day being unusually hot, the prince thought it
best to encamp there, and proposed it to Badoura,

who having the same wish the more readily
consented. They alighted in one of the finest
spots; a tent was presently set up, and the princess, weary with the fatigues of the journey, bade
her women untie her girdle, which they laid
down by her, and she falling asleep, they left her
alone.

Kummir al Zummaun had been giving directions
to his attendants, and, having seen all things in
order, came to the tent where the princess was
sleeping he entered, and sat down without making
any noise, intending to repose himself but observing
the princess's girdle lying by her, he took it up
and looked at the diamonds and rubies one by one.
In viewing it he observed a little purse hanging to
it, sewed neatly on the stuff, and tied fast with a
riband; he felt it and found it contained something
solid. Desirous to know what it was, he opened
the purse, and took out a cornelian engraven with
unknown figures and characters. "This cornelian,"
said the prince, "must be something very valuable,
or my princess would not carry it with so much
care." It was Badoura's talisman, which the Queen
of China had given her daughter as a charm that
would keep her, as she said, from any harm as long
as she had it about her.

The prince, the better to look at the talisman,
took it out to the light, the tent being dark; and
while he was holding it up in his hand, a bird

darted down from the air and snatched it away
from him.

Great was the concern and grief of the prince
when he saw the bird fly away with the talisman,
he followed the bird, which
settled on the ground not
far off, with the talisman
in its beak. The prince
drew near, hoping it would
drop it; but as he approached, the
bird took wing, and settled again
on the ground further off. He
followed, the bird took a further
flight. the prince, being very dexter-
ous at a mark, thought to kill it
with a stone, and still pursued; the
further it flew, the more eager he
grew in pursuing, keeping it always
in view. Thus the bird drew him
along from hill to valley, and valley
to hill, all the day, every step leading him out of the way from the

A bird snatched the
talisman from him.

plain where he had left his camp
and the Princess Badoura, and instead of perching at night on a bush, where he
might probably have taken it, roosted on a high
tree, safe from his pursuit. The prince, vexed to
the heart at having taken so much pains, and yet
not recovered the talisman, determined to rest where

he was until the morning. "For," said he, "how shall I find my way back across hills and valleys in the darkness?"

So he lay down beneath a tree and soon fell fast asleep. He awoke the next morning before the bird had left the tree, and as soon as he saw it on the wing, he followed it again the whole of that day, with no better success than he had done the last, eating nothing but herbs and fruits as he went. He did the same for ten days together, pursuing the bird, and keeping it in view from morning to night, lying always under the tree where it roosted.

On the eleventh day the bird continued flying, and Kummir al Zummaun pursuing it came near a great city. When the bird reached the walls, it flew over them, and the prince saw no more of it; so that he despaired of ever recovering the Princess Badoura's talisman.

He went into the city, which was built on the sea-shore and had a fine port, and walked up and down the streets without knowing where he was, or where to stop.

At last he came to the port, in as great uncertainty as ever as to what he should do. Walking along the shore, he perceived the gate of a garden open, and an old gardener at work in it; the good man, looking up, saw he was a stranger and a Mussulman, and asked him to come in and shut the door after him.

When the bird reached the walls, it flew over them, and the prince saw no more of it.

Kummir al Zummaun entered and demanded of
the gardener why he was so cautious. "Because,"
replied the old man, "I see you are a stranger newly
arrived; and this city is inhabited for the most part
by idolators, who have a mortal aversion to us

Mussulmen, and treat the
few of us that are here
with great barbarity. I suppose you did not know this,
and it is a miracle that you
have escaped as you have
thus far." Then the worthy
man took the prince into his
little hut, saying, "Come in,
and rest." And after he
had set a meal before him
and the prince had eaten
heartily, he requested him
to relate how he had come
there.

*Kummir al Zummaun entered
the garden.*

The prince complied, and when he had finished
his story he asked the nearest route to his father's
territories. "For," said he, "it is in vain for me to
think of finding my princess where I left her, after
wandering for eleven days from the spot."

The gardener replied that it was a year's journey
from that city to any country inhabited by Mussulmen; that the quickest passage for him would be to
go to the Isle of Ebene, whence he might easily

transport himself to the Isles of the Children of
Khaledan, that a ship sailed from the port every
year to Ebene, but that unfortunately one had
departed but a few days ago. "Had you come a
little sooner," said the gardener, "you might have
taken your passage in it. Now you must wait till it
makes the voyage again, and if you will stay with
me and accept of my house, such as it is, you shall
be as welcome to it as to your own."

The prince gladly accepted the gardener's offer,
and abode with him that year, working in the garden
by day, and passing the night in sighs, tears and
complaints, thinking of his dear Princess Badoura.

Meanwhile the princess was wondering what had
become of the prince. When she awoke, after a long
sleep, and found the prince was not with her, she
called her women, and asked if they knew where he
was. They had seen him enter the tent, but no one
had seen him go out.

While they were talking to her, she took up
her girdle, found her little purse open and her talisman gone. She did not doubt the prince had taken
it to see what it was, and that he would bring it
back with him. She waited impatiently for his
return, unable to imagine what made him stay away
from her so long.

When night fell she was overcome with grief,
and heartily wished she had never possessed the
talisman, as it seemed that the loss of it was the

*The princess continued the journey under the name of
Kummir al Zummaun.*

cause of her trouble. However, she did not lose
her judgment, but came to a very courageous resolution.

Only herself and her women knew of the prince's
absence, for his men were reposing or asleep in their
tents; but she was afraid that if it became known
she might find some difficulty in controlling men,
who would possibly refuse to submit to a woman.
She therefore laid aside her own habit, and put on
one of Kummir al Zummaun's. She was so much
like him, that the next day, when she came abroad,
the male attendants took her for the prince.

18

She commanded them to pack up their baggage
and begin their march, and when all things were
ready, she ordered one of her women to go into her
litter, she herself mounting on horseback and riding
by her side. They travelled several months by land
and sea, the princess continuing the journey under
the name of Kummir al Zummaun. They touched
at Ebene on their way to the Isles of the Children
of Khaledan, and went to the capital, where a king
reigned whose name was Armanos.

As soon as King Armanos heard of the arrival
of Prince Kummir al Zummaun, he waited upon him,
accompanied by his courtiers.

He received the disguised princess as the son
of a king who was his friend, and with whom he
always kept up a good understanding: he conducted
her to the palace, where an apartment was prepared
for her and all her attendants, though she would fain
have excused herself. He showed her all possible
honour and entertained her three days together with
extraordinary magnificence.

At the end of this time, King Armanos, understanding that the princess intended proceeding on
her voyage, charmed with the air and qualities of
such an accomplished prince, as he supposed her,
suggested that she should remain at Ebene, marry
his only daughter, and accept the crown, which he
was willing to resign in her favour.

"It is time for me to rest," said he, "and nothing

could be a greater pleasure to me in my retirement, than to see my people ruled by so worthy a successor to my throne."

The poor princess was afraid to own she was not Prince Kummir al Zummaun, and equally afraid to decline the honour he offered her lest, being so much bent upon the marriage, his kindness might turn to aversion, and he might take her life

These considerations determined her to accept the proposal of King Armanos and marry his daughter

The marriage treaty being thus concluded, the ceremony was put off till the next day.

In the meantime she gave notice to her officers and men, who still took her for their prince, that, with the Princess Badoura's consent, she was about to wed the Princess Haiatalnefous.

There was nothing very extraordinary in this, because in those countries it is usual for a man to have two wives. She talked to her women and bade them keep the secret, after which she took the Princess Haiatalnefous into her confidence, and promised her that when the real prince arrived, he would most certainly wed her if she had a mind to take him.

On these conditions the princess agreed to keep the secret, and the marriage ceremony was carried out with all due magnificence, and the Princess Badoura rose in the king's esteem and affection, and governed the kingdom peaceably and prosperously.

While things were thus passing in the Isle of
Ebene, Prince Kummir al Zummaun remained in the
city of idolators with the gardener.

One morning early, as the prince was walking
in the garden, the noise which two birds were making
on a neighbouring tree led him to lift up his head
to see what was the matter. The two birds were
fighting furiously, and in a very little while one of
them fell down dead at the foot of the tree; the
victorious bird took wing again, and flew away.

In an instant, two other large birds, that had
beheld the battle at a distance, came from the other
side of the garden, and pitched on the ground, one
at the feet, and the other at the head of the dead
bird they looked at it for some time, shaking their
heads in token of grief, after which they dug a grave
with their talons and buried it.

They then flew away, but returned in a few
minutes, bringing with them the bird that had
committed the murder, one holding one of its wings
in its beak, and the other one of its legs, the criminal
all the while crying out in a doleful manner and
struggling to escape.

They carried it to the grave of the bird which
it had lately sacrificed and there killed it, leaving
the body on the spot unburied, and flew away.

The prince beheld this singular spectacle in
astonishment, and drawing near the tree cast his
eyes upon the remains of the dead bird, amongst

which he spied something red. He took it up and found it was his beloved Princess Badoura's talisman, the loss of which had cost him so much pain and sorrow.

It is impossible to describe the prince's joy. He kissed the talisman, wrapped it in a riband, and tied it carefully about his arm. Shortly after this the good gardener bade him root up an old tree which bore no fruit. Kummir al Zummaun took an axe and began his work. In cutting off a branch of the root he found his axe strike against something that resisted the blow. He removed the earth, and discovered a broad plate of brass, under which was a staircase of ten steps.

He removed the earth and discovered a broad plate of brass.

He went down, and at the bottom saw a cavity about six yards square, with fifty brass urns placed in order, each with a cover over it. He opened them all, one after another, and found they were all full of gold-dust. He came out of the cave, rejoicing that he had found such a vast treasure, put the brass on the staircase, and rooted up the tree against the gardener's return.

When he came in he told the prince that he

had just learned that a ship was about to sail for the Isle of Ebene in a few days' time, and that he had arranged with the captain for the prince's passage.

"You could not bring me more agreeable tidings," said the prince, "and in return, I have also tidings that will be as welcome to you come along with me and you shall see what good fortune heaven has in store for you"

The prince led the gardener to the place where he had rooted up the tree, made him go down into the cave, and showed him the treasure.

"These riches are not mine," said the gardener, "the property is yours I have no right to it. For fourscore years, since my father's death, I have dug in this garden without discovering it; clearly it was destined for you."

But Kummir al Zummaun would not be surpassed in generosity by the gardener, and protested he would have none of the treasure unless it were shared by his friend.

The good man, to please the prince, consented, so they shared it between them, and each had twenty-five urns

Having done this the gardener advised the prince to be careful to get his treasure privately on board. "Otherwise you will run the risk of losing it," said he. "Olives are exported from here to Ebene. you know I have plenty of them. take what you will, fill fifty pots, half with the gold-dust and

half with olives, and I will get them carried to the
ship when you embark."

The prince followed this advice, and spent the
rest of the day in packing up the gold and the olives
in the fifty pots, and fearing the talisman, which he
wore on his arm, might be lost again, he carefully

He saw a cavity with fifty brass urns.

put it into one of the pots, with a particular mark
to distinguish it from the rest.

Now whether the gardener, who was a very old
man, was quite worn out with age, or had exhausted
himself too much that day, he was taken ill that
night, grew worse the next day, and on the third,
when the prince was ready to embark, was so ill
that it was plain he was near his end.

As soon as day broke, the captain of the ship came with several seamen to ask for the passenger who was to sail with them.

The prince told them to take the pots of olives and his baggage aboard, promising to follow as soon as he had taken leave of the gardener.

The seamen took the pots and baggage and the captain bade the prince make haste, the wind being fair.

When the captain and his men were gone Kummir al Zummaun went to take leave of the gardener, and thank him for all his good offices, but found him dying; and had scarcely time to bid him rehearse the articles of his faith, which all good Mussulmen do before they die, when he expired.

The prince could do no less than remain to prepare him for burial and lay him in his grave, for there was no one else to do so, and it was almost evening before he had finished. He then ran with all his might to the water-side, but when he reached the port he found the ship had sailed several hours, and was already out of sight. It had waited for him three hours, and, the wind standing fair, the captain durst not stay longer

Kummir al Zummaun was exceedingly grieved at being forced to remain another year in a country where he neither had, nor wished to have, any acquaintance. But the greatest affliction of all was, his having parted with the Princess Badoura's talisman

The only course was to return to the garden, to rent it of the landlord, and to continue to cultivate it. He hired a boy to assist him in the drudgery, and that he might not lose the other half of the treasure, which came to him by the death of the gardener, who had no heirs, he put the gold-dust into fifty other jars, which he filled up with olives, to be ready against the ship's return.

While the prince was beginning another year of labour, sorrow and impatience, the ship was nearing the Isle of Ebene.

The palace being by the sea-shore, the new king, or rather the Princess Badoura, espying the ship as she was entering into the port, with all her flags flying, asked what vessel it was, and hearing that it came yearly from the city of the idolators and was generally richly laden, went down to the port just as the captain came ashore. She questioned him closely, hoping to hear some news of Kummir al Zummaun, but she was disappointed in this, for the captain told her he had no passengers on board, only merchants who had with them rich stuffs, linens, diamonds, musks, spices, olives and many other articles.

The Princess Badoura loved olives exceedingly, and she at once ordered the captain to land what he had, and she would take them off his hands.

"Sire," replied the captain, "there are fifty great jars of olives, but they belong to a merchant whom I was forced to leave behind."

"No matter," answered the princess, "bring them ashore; we will nevertheless make a bargain for them."

The captain demanded one thousand pieces of silver, but, hearing that the merchant was very poor, the princess ordered one thousand pieces of gold to be given to the captain for the olive merchant.

The money was paid, and the jars carried to the palace.

Night drawing on, the princess withdrew into the inner palace, and went to the Princess Haiatalnefous' apartment, ordering the olives to be brought thither. She opened one jar, to let the Princess Haiatalnefous taste them, and poured them into a dish. Great was her astonishment when she found the olives were mingled with gold-dust. She ordered the women to open and empty all the jars in her presence, and her wonder was still greater when she saw that the olives in all of them were mixed with gold-dust; but when she saw her talisman drop out, she was so surprised that she fainted away.

However, she soon recovered herself and told the Princess Haiatalnefous the cause of her agitation.

The next day, as soon as it was light, she sent for the captain of the ship and asked him many questions about the merchant to whom the olives belonged, but he knew very little of him, except that he worked in a garden and seemed very poor So the princess next ordered him to set sail that very day for the city of idolators, and to go with all speed and fetch the olive merchant and bring him to her, threatening that if he did not do so his life and the lives of all with him should be confiscated.

So the captain lost no time in carrying out his orders. He had a prosperous voyage to the city, and when he went ashore took with him six stout seamen They at once went to the garden of Kummir al Zummaun, took hold of him and carried him on board, and set sail for the Isle of Ebene.

Kummir al Zummaun asked the captain why he was thus taken by force, and when the captain told him it was by the orders of the King of Ebene he was very much surprised, in that he had never set foot in his kingdom before and did not know him.

The captain was not long on his voyage back to the Isle of Ebene. Though it was night when he cast anchor in the port, he landed immediately, and, taking his prisoner with him, hastened to the palace, where he demanded to be introduced to the king.

The Princess Badoura had withdrawn into the inner palace, but when she heard of the captain's return she came out to speak to him, and as soon as she saw the prince, though he was in his gardener's dress, she recognised him Although she was longing to embrace him, she knew it was for the interest of both of them that she should act the king a little longer before she made herself known.

She turned to the captain and gave him a rich diamond, worth much more than the expense he had been put to for both voyages. She also bade him keep the thousand pieces of gold she had given for the olives, telling him she would make up the account with the merchant whom he had brought with him.

She ordered Kummir al Zummaun to be clothed in rich apparel and to be carefully tended by one of her officers, and then sent for him to her apartment, and, dismissing her attendants, shut the door and produced the talisman. "It is not long since an astrologer presented it to me," she said, "you, being skilful in all things, may perhaps tell me its use."

Kummir al Zummaun took the talisman, and drew near a lamp to view it. As soon as he recognised it he said, "Sire, the use of this talisman is to kill me with grief and despair if I do not quickly find the most charming and lovely princess in the world, to whom it belonged"

"You shall tell me the particulars another time," replied the pretended king; "remain here a little and I will soon return to you."

At these words she retired, put off her royal turban, and in a few minutes dressed herself in her female attire, and having the girdle round her which she had on the day of their separation.

Kummir al Zummaun immediately recognised

his dear princess, ran to her and tenderly embraced her, exclaiming · "How much am I obliged to the king who has so agreeably surprised me."

"Do not expect to see the king any more," replied the princess, embracing him in her turn · "you see him in me, sit down and I will explain."

They seated themselves, and the princess explained all that had happened to her, how she had thought it best for her safety to pass herself off as Kummir al Zummaun, and how she had been obliged to marry the Princess Haiatalnefous, who had helped her to keep the secret.

The prince in his turn related all his adventures.

The next morning, as soon as it was light, the Princess Badoura dressed herself in her female attire and sent the chief of the guards to King Armanos, to desire he would oblige her by coming to her apartment.

When the king entered the apartment he was amazed to see a lady who was unknown to him, and he at once asked where the king was.

The princess answered. "Yesterday I was king, but to-day I am only Princess of China, wife to the true Prince Kummir al Zummaun If your Majesty will have patience to hear our adventures, I hope you will not condemn me for putting an innocent deceit upon you." The king bade her go on, and heard her narrative from beginning to end with astonishment. The princess on finishing said: "Sire,

as you know it is the custom with most men to
have several wives, I trust your Majesty will consent
to give your daughter, the Princess Haiatalnefous,
in marriage to the prince; I will with all my heart
yield up to her the rank and quality of queen, which
of right belongs to her, and content myself with the
second place."

King Armanos turned to Kummir al Zummaun
and said "Son, since the Princess Badoura your
wife, whom I have all along thought to be my son-
in-law, assures me that she is willing for my daughter
to become your wife, I would know if you are
willing to marry her and accept the crown."

"Sire," replied Kummir al Zummaun, "though
I desire nothing so earnestly as to see the king my
father, yet the obligations I have to your Majesty
and the Princess Haiatalnefous are so weighty, I can
refuse her nothing "

The prince was then proclaimed king, and married
the same day with all possible demonstrations of joy,
and had every reason to be well pleased with the
beauty and wit of the Princess Haiatalnefous.

The two queens lived together afterwards on the
most friendly and cordial terms.

Some time afterwards news was brought to
Kummir al Zummaun that a large army was approaching his capital, and upon sending messengers to go
and see what army it was, he learned that it belonged
to his dear father Shaw Zummaun, who had left the

Isles of the Children of Khaledan and who had travelled a long time in search of his son.

Kummir al Zummaun at once went out to meet his father, and never was a more affecting interview than when they met.

Shaw Zummaun gently upbraided his son with unkindness in so cruelly leaving him, and Kummir al Zummaun confessed hearty sorrow for the fault which love had urged him to commit.

SINDBAD THE SAILOR.

Hindbad.

IN the reign of the Caliph Haroun al Reschid there lived at Bagdad a poor porter called Hindbad. One day, whilst carrying a very heavy load, he sat down to rest for a few moments in the porch of a magnificent house in which lived a famous voyager named Sindbad. Hearing the sounds of feasting and laughter, he exclaimed aloud:

"Consider the difference between Sindbad and me. I am every day exposed to fatigues and calamities, and can scarcely get coarse barley-bread for myself and my family, whilst happy Sindbad expends immense riches and leads a life of continual pleasure. What has he done to obtain a lot so agreeable? And what have I done to deserve one so wretched?"

It chanced that Sindbad overheard the porter's words and, sending for him into his house, first feasted him well and then related to him the following strange adventures.

"I inherited from my father," said he, "considerable property; but having squandered the greater part in my youth it became necessary for me to find a means of making a livelihood. I decided to enter into a contract with some merchants who traded by sea. I accordingly went to Bussorah and embarked with several merchants on board a ship which we had jointly fitted out.

"We set sail and steered our course towards the Indies, through the Persian Gulf. At first I was troubled with sea-sickness, but speedily recovered my health, and was not afterwards subject to that complaint.

"In our voyage we touched at several islands where we sold or exchanged our goods. One day we were becalmed near a small island, but little elevated above the level of the water, and resembling a green meadow. The captain ordered his sails to be furled, and permitted such persons as were inclined to land. I was amongst the number, and while we were enjoying ourselves in eating and drinking, and recovering ourselves from the fatigue of the sea, the island on a sudden trembled, and shook us terribly.

"The captain, perceiving what had happened, called upon us to re-embark, or we should all be lost, for what we took for an island proved to be the back of a sea monster.

19

"The nimblest got into the sloop, others betook themselves to swimming; but for myself I was still upon the back of the creature when he dived into the sea, and I had only time to catch hold of a piece of wood that we had brought out of the ship to make a fire.

"Meanwhile the captain, believing me to have perished, set sail, a favourable breeze having sprung up.

"Thus was I exposed to the mercy of the waves and struggled for my life all the rest of the day and the following night, when, just as my strength was failing me, a wave threw me up upon a seemingly uninhabited island.

"But fortunately for me it chanced that the island, which was very extensive, was not uninhabited, but the end at which I had been cast up, being very bleak and desolate, was seldom visited by the natives. The maharaja who owned the island, having lost some valuable horses, had sent some of his grooms in search of them, and these men had penetrated as far as the point upon which I had been cast up. They soon discovered me and, having heard my story, gave me some provisions and invited me to return with them the following day to the capital of the island.

"The maharaja received me with great kindness and gave orders that I should be furnished with all I required. The maharaja's capital being situated on the sea coast and having a fine harbour, I

frequented the company of men of my own pro-
fession, hoping to hear news from Bagdad, or find
an opportunity to return.

"As I was one day at the port a ship arrived,
and as soon as she cast anchor they began to un-
load her, and the goods
were carried on shore to
be sold. Judge then of
my surprise when I per-
ceived some of the bales
to be the same I had
embarked at Bussorah. I
went on board and made
myself known to the cap-
tain, who embraced me
with great joy. 'Heaven
be praised,' said he, 'for
your happy escape. I can-
not express the joy it affords

*Sindbad was exposed to the mercy
of the waves.*

me: there are your goods, take and do with them as
you please.'

"I took out what was most valuable in my bales
and presented them to the maharaja, who, knowing
my misfortune, asked me how I came by such rarities. I acquainted him with the circumstances of
their recovery. He was pleased with my good luck,
accepted my present, and in return gave me one
much more considerable. Upon this I took leave
of him, and went aboard the same ship, after I had

exchanged my goods for wood of aloes, sandal, camphire, nutmegs, cloves, pepper, ginger and other commodities of that country. We arrived safely at Bussorah, where I sold my goods for a hundred thousand sequins and returned to Bagdad.

"I designed after my first voyage to spend the rest of my days at Bagdad, but it was not long before I grew tired of an indolent life. My inclination to trade revived. I bought goods proper for the commerce I intended, and put to sea a second time with merchants of known probity We traded from island to island and exchanged commodities with great profit. One day we landed on an island covered with several sorts of fruit trees, but we could see neither man nor animal. We wandered about the meadows and beside the streams, and presently I sat down in a shady spot, with my wine and provisions beside me, and soon fell fast asleep I cannot tell how long I slept, but when I awoke the ship was gone I leave you to guess my melancholy reflections in this sad condition. I upbraided myself a hundred times for not being content with the produce of my first voyage, that might have sufficed me all my life. But all this was in vain, and my repentance too late.

"At last I resigned myself and, not knowing what to do, I climbed up to the top of a lofty tree, from whence I looked about on all sides. When I gazed towards the sea I could see nothing but sky and water, but looking over the land I beheld something white; so coming down, I took what provision I had left, and went towards it, the distance being so great that I could not distinguish what it was.

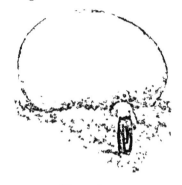

As I approached, I took it to be a white dome of a prodigious height and extent, and when I came up to it, I touched it, and found it to be very smooth. I went round to see if it was open on any side, but saw it was not, and that there was no climbing up to the top as it was so smooth. It was at least fifty paces round

The roc's egg.

"By this time the sun was about to set, and all of a sudden the sky became as dark as if it had been covered with a thick cloud I was much astonished at this sudden darkness, but much more so when I found it occasioned by a bird of monstrous size, that came flying towards me. I remembered that I had often heard mariners speak of a miraculous bird called 'roc,' and conceived that the great dome which I so much admired must be its egg, for the bird alighted and sat over it, and as I crept closer I found the bird's legs were as big as the trunk of a tree.

"I tied myself to one of them with the cloth of

my turban in hopes that the roc next morning would
carry me with her out of this desert island, nor was
I mistaken, for in the morning as soon as it was
daylight she flew away, first to a great height, and
then descended with such rapidity that I lost my
senses. As soon as I found myself on the ground,
I speedily untied the knot, and had scarcely done
so when the roc, having taken up a serpent of monstrous length in her bill, flew away again.

"The spot where it left me was encompassed on
all sides by mountains that seemed to reach above
the clouds, and so steep that there was no possibility
of getting out of the valley. This was a new perplexity so that when I compared this place with
the desert island from which the roc had brought
me, I found that I had gained nothing by the change.

"As I walked through this valley I perceived that
it was strewn with diamonds, some of which were of
a surprising size; but the satisfaction the sight caused
me was somewhat diminished by some other objects
I presently saw at a distance, namely, a great number
of serpents, so large that the least of them was capable
of swallowing an elephant. I spent the day in walking
about the valley, and when night came on I went
into a cave, where I thought I might repose in safety.
I secured the entrance, which was low and narrow,
with a great stone to preserve me from the serpents,
without excluding the light. I supped on part of my
provisions, but the serpents, which began hissing round

me, put me into such extreme fear that I could not sleep.

"When day appeared the serpents retired and I came out of the cave trembling, but as I had not dared to sleep during the night, I presently fell asleep and was awakened by something falling by me with a great noise.

"This proved to be a large piece of raw meat; and at the same time I saw several others fall down from the rocks in different places.

"I had always regarded as fabulous what I had heard sailors and others relate of the valley of diamonds, and of the stratagems employed by merchants to obtain jewels from thence; but now I found that they had stated nothing but the truth. For the fact is, the merchants come to the neighbourhood of this valley when the eagles have young ones, and, throwing great joints of meat into the valley, the diamonds, upon whose points they fall, stick to them; then the eagles, which are stronger in this country than anywhere else, pounce with great force upon those pieces of meat, and carry them to their nests on the precipices of the rocks to feed their young. the merchants then run to the nests, drive off the eagles and take away the diamonds that stick to the meat.

"Until I perceived the device I had concluded it to be impossible for me to get from this abyss, but now I changed my opinion and began to think upon the means of my deliverance. I began to collect together the largest diamonds I could find, and put them into the leather bag in which I used to carry my provisions. I afterwards took the largest of the pieces of meat, tied it close round me with the cloth of my turban, and then laid myself upon the ground with my face downward, the bags of diamonds being made fast to my girdle. I had scarcely placed myself in this posture when the eagles came.

"Each of them seized a piece of meat, and one of the strongest, having taken me up with the meat to which I was fastened, carried me to his nest on the top of the mountain.

"The merchants immediately began their shouting to frighten the eagles, and when they had obliged them to quit their prey one of them came to the nest where I was. He was much alarmed when he saw me; but recovering himself asked me how I came thither. I was explaining to him the manner of my deliverance from the valley, when the other merchants came crowding about us, much astonished to see me, but much more surprised when I told them my story. They conducted me to their encampment and then, having opened my bag, they were surprised at the largeness of my diamonds, and confessed that in all the Courts which they had visited they had never seen any of such size and perfection. I prayed the merchant who owned the

One of the merchants came to the nest where I was.

nest to which I had been carried (for every merchant had his own) to take as many for his share as he pleased. He contented himself with one, and that too the least of them, and when I pressed him to take more, without fear of doing me any injury, 'No,' said he, 'I am very well satisfied with this, which is valuable enough to save me the trouble of making any more voyages, and will raise as great a fortune as I desire.'

"I spent several days with the merchants, and every day they threw their pieces of meat into the valley, until, being satisfied with the diamonds they had gathered, we left the place, travelling near high mountains, where there were serpents of a prodigious length, which we had the good fortune to escape. We took shipping at the first port we reached, and touched at the island of Roha, where the trees grow that yield camphire. This tree is so large, and its branches so thick, that one hundred men may easily sit under its shade. In this island is also found the rhinoceros, an animal less in size than the elephant, but larger than the buffalo. It has a horn upon its nose, about a cubit in length; this horn is solid, and when cleft through the middle white lines may be seen, which represent the figure of a man.

"At this island I exchanged some of my diamonds for merchandise, with which I traded at the other ports we touched at, until at length we

landed at Bussorah, from whence I proceeded to
Bagdad.

"I soon lost in the pleasures of life the remem-
brance of the perils I had encountered in my two
former voyages, and soon grew weary of living
without business, and therefore travelled to Bussorah,
carrying with me some of the richest commodities
with which to trade. But this voyage proved as
adventurous and full of dangers as the last. For
being overtaken with a storm in mid-ocean, we were
driven from our course and forced to cast anchor in
the port of an island which was inhabited by hairy
savages. These attacked us in such numbers that
we were unable to resist them. They took possession
of our ship and all that it contained and carried it
away to another island, leaving us in a sorry plight,
for we soon discovered that we were in the power
of a terrible giant, who set about making preparations to kill and cook us all. But fortunately there
was an abundance of floating timber near the island,
and whilst the giant was at work we succeeded in
building a number of rafts upon which we made our
escape.

"But alas! our enemy soon discovered what had
happened, and bringing two other giants to help him
they took up great stones, and running into the water
they threw them with such unerring aim that all the
rafts except the one I was on were sunk. But still
my good fortune did not desert me, for after passing

through terrible dangers, first by sea and then by
land, the sea having cast my raft upon an island inhabited only by enormous serpents, I was mercifully
preserved from these terrible pests, and succeeded
in attracting the attention of a passing ship, which
took me off the island and
carried me safely home.

"But my passion for
trade and love of novelty
again prevented my settling
down quietly at Bagdad, and
it was not long before I
embarked upon my fourth
voyage.

"This was no less dis-
astrous than the former ones.
Our good ship was caught
by a tremendous gale and
driven on shore, many of the
merchants and seamen were
drowned and the cargo was

Sindbad succeeded in attracting
the attention of a passing ship.

lost. Once again did I fall into the power of canni-
bals, but since I was very thin and lean they spared my
life, intending to fatten me. However, I managed to
escape from them and had the good fortune to meet
with a tribe of people who treated me very kindly,
so kindly indeed that they did not wish me to leave
them, and I abode with them many years, teaching
them many handicrafts, such as saddle-making, of

which they knew nothing, but for the knowledge of which they paid me so handsomely that I grew very prosperous.

"But I could not reconcile myself to remaining away from my own country permanently, and after a very long time I succeeded in getting away and returned to Bagdad. I carried with me great stores of precious stones and rich merchandise, out of which I did not fail to contribute liberally towards the support of several mosques, and the subsistence of the poor.

"The pleasures I enjoyed in the society of my kindred and friends soon made me forget all the troubles and calamities I had undergone, but did not cure me of my inclination to make new voyages After a certain time I therefore bought goods and, having built a ship, I set sail in her with several other merchants of different nations who had agreed to sail with me.

"We sailed with the first fair wind and, after a long navigation, the first place we touched at was a desert island, where we found an egg of a roc, equal in size to that I formerly mentioned. There was a young roc in it just ready to be hatched, and its bill had begun to appear. The merchants who had landed with me broke the egg with hatchets, made a hole in it, and pulled out the young roc piecemeal and roasted it. I had earnestly entreated them not to meddle with the egg, but they would not listen to me. Scarcely had they finished their repast, when there appeared in the air, at a considerable distance from us, two great clouds. The captain whom I had hired to navigate the ship, knowing by experience what they meant, said they were the male and female roc that belonged to the young one, and pressed us

to re-embark with all speed to prevent the misfortune which he saw would otherwise befall us. We hastened on board and set sail with all possible speed.

"In the meantime, the two rocs approached with a frightful noise, which they redoubled when they saw the egg broken and their young one gone. They flew back in the direction from which they had come, and dis-

By the dexterity of the steersman it missed us.

appeared for some time, while we made all the sail we could to endeavour to prevent that which unhappily befell us.

"They returned, and we observed that each of them carried between its talons stones, or rather rocks, of a monstrous size.

"When they came directly over my ship, they hovered, and one of them let fall a rock, but by the dexterity of the steersman it missed us and, falling into the sea, divided the water so that we could almost see the bottom. The other roc, to our misfortune, threw his burden so exactly upon the middle of the ship as to split it into a thousand pieces. The mariners and passengers were all crushed to death or sunk.

"I myself was of the number of the latter, but as I came up again I fortunately caught hold of a piece of the wreck, and swimming sometimes with one hand, and sometimes with the other, but always holding fast my board, the wind and tide favouring me, I came to an island whose shore was very steep. I overcame that difficulty, however, and got ashore.

"I sat down upon the grass to recover myself from my fatigue, after which I went into the island to explore it. It seemed to be a delicious garden I found trees everywhere, some of them bearing fruits, and there were streams of fresh pure water, which was light and good to drink

"As I advanced into the island, I saw an old man, who appeared very weak and infirm. He was sitting on the bank of a stream, and at first I took him to be one who had been shipwrecked like myself. I went towards him and saluted him, but he only slightly bowed his head. I asked him why he sat so still, but instead of answering me, he made a sign for me to take him upon my back, and carry him over the brook, signifying he wished to gather fruit

"I believed he really stood in need of my assistance, took him upon my back, and having carried
him over, bade him get down, and for that end
stooped that he might get off with ease; but instead
of doing so the old man, who to me appeared quite
decrepit, clasped his legs nimbly about my neck.

Sindbad went towards him and saluted him.

He sat astride upon my shoulders and held my throat
so tight that I thought he would have strangled me,
the apprehension of which made me swoon. Notwithstanding my fainting the ill-natured old fellow
kept fast about my neck, but opened his legs a little
to give me time to recover my breath. When I
had done so he struck me so rudely with his feet

that I was forced to rise. He made me walk under the trees, and forced me now and then to stop to gather and eat fruit such as we found.

"He never left me all day, and when I lay down to rest at night, laid himself down with me, holding always fast about my neck Every morning he pushed me to make me awake and afterwards obliged me to get up and walk. You may judge then what trouble I was in to be loaded with such a burden of which I could not get rid.

"One day I found several dry calabashes that had fallen from a tree. I took a large one, and, after cleaning it, pressed into it some juice of grapes, which abounded in the island; having filled the calabash, I put it by in a convenient place, and going thither again some days after, I tasted it and found the wine so good that it soon made me forget my sorrow, gave me new vigour, and so exhilarated my spirits that I began to sing and dance as I walked along.

"The old man perceiving the effect which this liquor had upon me, and that I carried him with more ease than before, made me a sign to give him some of it I handed him the calabash and, the liquor pleasing his palate, he drank it all off. There being a considerable quantity of it, he became intoxicated and began to sing after his manner, and to dance upon my shoulders. He loosened his legs by degrees and I threw him

upon the ground, where he lay without motion; I then took up a great stone and crushed his head to pieces.

"I was extremely glad to be thus freed for ever from this troublesome fellow. I walked towards the beach, where I met the crew of a ship that had cast anchor to take in water. They were surprised to see me, but more so at hearing the particulars of my adventures. 'You fell,' they said, 'into the hands of the old man of the sea, and are the first who ever escaped strangling by his malicious tricks. He never quitted those he had once made himself master of, till he had destroyed them, and he has made this island notorious by the number of men he has slain; so that the merchants and mariners who landed upon it durst not advance into the island, unless they were in great numbers.'

"After having informed me of these things, they carried me with them to the ship; the captain received me with great kindness when they told him what had befallen me. He put out again to sea, and after some days' sail we arrived at the harbour of a great city, the houses of which were built with hewn stone.

"One of the merchants, who had taken me into his friendship, invited me to go along with him, and carried me to a place appointed for the accommodation of foreign merchants. He gave me

20*

a large bag, and having recommended me to some
people of the town who were in the habit of
gathering cocoa-nuts, desired of them to take me
with them.

"We started and came presently to a forest of
cocoa-nut trees, very lofty and with trunks so smooth
that it was not possible to climb to the branches
that bore the fruit. When we entered the forest we
saw a great number of apes of several sizes, who fled
as soon as they perceived us, and climbed to the top
of the trees with surprising swiftness. The merchants
with whom I was collected stones and threw them
at the apes. I did the same, and the apes, out of
revenge, threw cocoa-nuts at us so fast, and with
such gestures as sufficiently testified their anger and
resentment. We gathered up the cocoa-nuts, and
from time to time threw stones to provoke the apes;
so that by this stratagem we filled our bags with
cocoa-nuts, which it would have been impossible
otherwise to have done.

"When we had gathered our number, we returned
to the city, where the merchant who had sent me to
the forest gave me the value of the cocoa-nuts I
brought. 'Go on,' said he, 'and do the like every day,
until you have got money enough to carry you home.'
I thanked him for his advice and gradually collected
as many cocoa-nuts as produced me a considerable
sum of money. I had likewise a number of cocoa-
nuts which I took with me upon the vessel on which

I embarked, and when she was ready to sail I took leave of the merchant who had been so kind to me.

"We sailed towards the islands where pepper grows in great plenty. From thence we went to the Isle of Comari, where the best species of wood of aloes grows. I exchanged my cocoa-nuts in those two islands for pepper and wood of aloes, and went with other merchants a pearl-fishing. I hired divers, who brought me up some that were very large and pure. Next I embarked in a vessel that happily arrived at Bussorah; from thence I returned to Bagdad, where I made vast sums of my pepper, wood of aloes and pearls. I gave the tenth of my gains in alms as I had done upon my return from my other voyages, and endeavoured to dissipate my fatigues by amusements of different kinds.

"One would have imagined that after being shipwrecked five times and escaped so many dangers, I should have resolved never again to tempt fortune and expose myself to new hardships. But after a year's rest I began to prepare for a sixth voyage.

"I travelled once more through several provinces of Persia and the Indies and arrived at a sea-port where I embarked in a ship bound on a long voyage. It was long indeed, and at the same time so unfortunate that the captain and pilot lost their course. They, however, at last discovered where they were, but we had no reason to rejoice at the circumstance. Suddenly we saw the captain quit his post, uttering loud lamentations. He threw off his turban, pulled his beard, and beat his head like a madman. We asked him the reason, and he answered that he was in the most dangerous place in all the ocean.

"A rapid current had caught the ship and it was carried to the foot of an inaccessible mountain where it struck and went to pieces, yet in such a manner that we saved our lives, our provisions, and the best of our goods.

"The mountain at the foot of which we were wrecked formed part of the coast of a very large island. It was covered with wrecks and we found an incredible quantity of goods and riches cast ashore. In all other places, rivers run from their channels into the sea, but here a river of fresh water runs out of the sea into a dark cavern, the entrance of which is very high and spacious. What is most remarkable in this place is, that the stones of the mountain are of crystal, rubies or other precious stones.

"Once cast ashore there is no escape from this terrible place, for the mountain is inaccessible and the strong current prevents escape by sea.

"At first we divided our provisions as equally as we could and thus everyone lived a longer or a shorter time, according to his strength; but death was inevitable and at length I was the only survivor of the party, and expecting almost hourly to breathe my last.

"But it pleased God once more to take com-

passion on me, and put it in my mind to go to the
bank of the river which ran into the great cavern.
Considering its probable course with great attention,
I said to myself, 'This river, which runs thus under-
ground, must somewhere have an issue. If I make
a raft, and leave myself to the current, it will convey
me to some inhabited country, or I shall perish. If
I be drowned, I lose nothing, but only change one
kind of death for another; and if I get out of this
fatal place, I shall not only avoid the sad fate of
my comrades, but perhaps find some new occasion
of enriching myself.'

"I immediately went to work upon large pieces
of timber and tied them together so strongly that I
soon made a very solid raft. When I had finished
I loaded it with rubies, emeralds, ambergris and
all other precious stones that were lying in that
place and went on board with two oars that I had
made.

"As soon as I entered the cavern I lost all light,
and the stream carried me I knew not whither. Thus
I floated some days in perfect darkness, and once
found the arch so low that it very nearly touched
my head. At length a stupor seized me; I cannot
tell how long it continued, but when I revived I was
surprised to find myself in an extensive plain on the
brink of a river, where my raft was tied, amidst a
great number of negroes.

"They spoke to me, but I did not understand

their language; but on my speaking a few words of Arabic one of the blacks came forward and answered me. He told me that he and his companions had been working in the fields when they observed my raft upon the river and brought it ashore He asked me to tell them my history and how I came to venture myself upon the river.

"Before satisfying their curiosity I begged for something to eat, and when my hunger was appeased I related all that had befallen me, which they listened to with attentive surprise, and then wished me to accompany them that I might go and tell my history to their king.

"As I was quite willing to go with them we marched till we came to the capital of Serendib, which was the name of the island in which I had landed.

"The king received me with great kindness and condescension, and when I had told all my history I caused the precious things I had brought with me on the raft to be brought in and straightway offered him the whole of my cargo

"But he would take nothing from me. He charged one of his officers to take care of me, and sent all my goods to a lodging provided for me.

"I spent a short time in the island and then begged the king to allow me to return home. He granted me permission in the most obliging and most honourable manner.

"He would needs force upon me a rich present, and when I went to take my leave of him he gave me a much more considerable present and a letter for the commander of the faithful, our sovereign, saying to me, 'I pray you give this present from me, and this letter, to the caliph, and assure him of my friendship'

"I took the present and the letter, thanked the king, and went on board a ship which set sail at once, and after a very successful navigation we landed at Bussorah, and from thence I went to Bagdad, where the first thing I did was to acquit myself of my commission.

"Being now safely returned from my sixth voyage I absolutely laid aside all thoughts of travelling; for, besides that my age now required rest, I was resolved no more to expose myself to such risks as I had encountered; so that I thought of nothing but to pass the rest of my days in tranquillity. One day as I was treating my friends, one of my servants came and told me, 'That an officer of the caliph wished to see me.' I rose from the table and went to him, and he requested me to accompany him forthwith to the caliph. This I did and having prostrated myself in the presence of our sovereign he said to me 'Sindbad, I stand in need of your service; you must carry my answer and a present to the king of Serendib. It is but just I should return his civility'

"This command of the caliph was to me like a clap of thunder. I had no wish ever to take another voyage, moreover I had made a vow never to go out of Bagdad

"But the caliph insisted upon my compliance and I was forced to submit. He ordered me one thousand sequins to pay for the expenses of my journey.

"I prepared for my departure in a few days, and as soon as the caliph's letter and present were delivered to me, I went to Bussorah, where I embarked and had a very happy voyage. Having arrived at Serendib I speedily executed my commission and as soon as I conveniently could solicited leave to depart, and had much difficulty to obtain it, so anxious was the king to keep me with him. When, however, I received permission, the king dismissed me with a very considerable present. I embarked immediately to return to Bagdad, but had not the good fortune to arrive there so speedily as I had hoped.

"Three or four days after my departure, we were attacked by pirates, who easily seized upon our ship, because it was no vessel of force. Some of the crew offered resistance which cost them their lives, but for myself and the rest, who were not so imprudent, the pirates saved us on purpose to make slaves of us.

"We were all stripped, and instead of our own

clothes they gave us sorry rags, and carried us into a remote island, where they sold us.

"I fell into the hands of a rich merchant, who, as soon as he bought me, carried me to his home, treated me well, and clad me handsomely for a slave. Some days after, not knowing who I was, he asked me if I understood any trade. I answered that I was no mechanic, but a merchant, and that the pirates who sold me had robbed me of all I possessed. 'But tell me,' replied he, 'can you shoot with a bow?' I answered that I could, and he gave me a bow and arrows and, taking me behind him upon an elephant, carried me to a thick forest some leagues from the town. Then showing me a great tree he bade me climb up into it and shoot at the elephants that passed by. It appeared there were a great number of them in that forest and my master was an ivory merchant.

"I remained in the tree all night without seeing any elephants; but in the morning I perceived a great number and succeeded in shooting one. The other elephants at once made off and I came down the tree and went to inform my master. He praised my dexterity and we returned to the forest together, where we dug a hole for the elephant, my patron meaning to return when it was rotten, and take his teeth to trade with

"I continued this employment for two months, and killed an elephant every day, getting sometimes upon one tree and sometimes upon another.

"One morning, as I looked for the elephants, I perceived with extreme amazement that, instead of passing by me as usual, they stopped and came to me with a horrible noise. They encompassed the tree in which I was concealed, with their trunks extended, and all fixed their eyes upon me. I was so alarmed that I allowed my bow and arrows to fall from my hands

"My fears were not without cause, for the largest elephant put his trunk round the foot of the tree, plucked it up, and threw it on the ground. I fell with the tree, and the elephant, taking me up with his trunk, laid me on his back, where I sat more like one dead than alive. He then put himself at the head of the other elephants, who followed him in troops, carried me a considerable way, and then laid me down on the ground and retired with all his companions. After seeing the elephants go I got up and found I was upon a long and broad hill, almost covered with the bones and teeth of elephants. This object furnished me with abundance of reflections. I admired the instinct of those animals, and doubted not but that this was their burying place, and that they carried me thither on purpose to tell me I should forbear to persecute them, since I did it only for their teeth I did not stay on the hill, but turned towards the city, and, after having travelled a day and a night, I came to my patron. I met no elephant on my way, which made me think they had retired

The elephant, taking Sindbad up, laid him upon his back.

farther into the forest, to leave me at liberty to
come back to the hill without any obstacle.

"As soon as my patron saw me he told me he
had been in great trouble to know what had become
of me. He had been into the forest and had found
a tree newly pulled up, and a bow and arrows on
the ground, and having sought for me in vain had
despaired of ever seeing me more.

"I told him all that had happened and we both
went the next morning to the hill.

"We loaded the elephant which had carried us
with as many teeth as he could bear, and when we

had returned my master said. 'Brother, for I will treat you no more as my slave, after having made such a discovery as will enrich me, I give you your liberty.'

"My master then told me what he had hitherto concealed from me. 'The elephants of our forest,' said he, 'have every year killed a great many of our slaves, whom we sent to seek ivory. For all the cautions we could give them, those crafty animals destroyed them one time or another. You only have escaped, and besides that have procured me incredible wealth. Formerly we could only procure ivory by exposing the lives of our slaves, and now our whole city is enriched by your means. Do not think I pretend to have rewarded you by giving you your liberty, I will also give you considerable riches.'

"'Your giving me my liberty is enough to discharge what you owe me,' I said, 'and I deserve no other reward for the service I had the good fortune to do to you and your city, but leave to return to my own country.'

"'Very well,' said he, 'the monsoon* will in a little time bring ships for ivory I will then send you home and give you money to pay your charges.'

"I stayed with him expecting the monsoon; and during that time we made so many journeys to the hill, that we filled all our warehouses with

---

* A regular wind that blows six months from the east, and as many from the west.

ivory. The other merchants who traded in it did the same, for it could not be long concealed from them.

"The ships arrived at last, and my patron, himself having made choice of the ship wherein I was to embark, loaded half of it with ivory on my account, laid in provisions in abundance for my passage, and besides obliged me to accept a present of some curiosities of the country of great value. After I had returned him a thousand thanks for all his favours, I went aboard.

"On our return voyage we stopped at some islands to take in fresh provisions. Our vessel being come to a port on the mainland in the Indies, we touched there, and not being willing to venture by sea to Bussorah, I landed my proportion of the ivory, resolving to proceed on my journey by land. I made vast sums of my ivory, bought several rarities, which I intended for presents, and when my equipage was ready, set out in company with a large caravan of merchants. I was a long time on the way, and suffered much, but endured all with patience, when I considered that I had nothing to fear from the sea, from pirates, from serpents, or from other perils to which I had been exposed. All these fatigues ended at last, and I arrived safely at Bagdad. I went immediately to wait upon the caliph, and gave him an account of my embassy, and moreover related to him all the surprising adventures I had met with.

"He deemed my adventures to be so curious, that he ordered one of his secretaries to write them in characters of gold, and lay them up in his treasury. I retired well satisfied with the honours I received, and the presents which he gave me; and ever since I have devoted myself wholly to my family, kindred and friends."

Sindbad here finished the relation of his seventh and last voyage, and then addressing himself to Hindbad, the porter, said

"Well, friend, did you ever hear of any person who suffered so much as I have done, or of any mortal that has gone through so many vicissitudes? Is it not reasonable that, after all this, I should enjoy a quiet and pleasant life?"

Hindbad drew near, and kissing his hand said "You not only deserve a quiet life, but are worthy of all the riches you enjoy, because you make of them such a good and generous use. May you therefore continue to live in happiness and joy till the day of your death."

Sindbad gave him one hundred sequins, received him into the number of his friends, desired him to quit his porter's employment, and come and dine every day with him, that he might have reason to remember Sindbad the Sailor.

THE STORY OF THE LITTLE HUNCHBACK.

The Hunchback.

THERE was in former times at Caspar, on the extreme boundaries of Tartary, a tailor who had a pretty wife, whom he affectionately loved, and by whom he was beloved with equal tenderness.

One day while he was at work, a little hunchback seated himself at the shop door and began to sing and play upon a tabor. The tailor was pleased with his performance, and resolved to take him to his house to entertain his wife. "This little fellow," said he, "will divert us both this evening." He accordingly invited him and the other readily accepted the invitation; so the tailor shut up his shop and carried him home. Immediately after their arrival, the tailor's wife placed before them a good

dish of fish, but as the little man was eating, he
unluckily swallowed a bone, which, notwithstanding
all that the tailor and his wife could do, choked
him

This accident greatly alarmed them both, for
they dreaded that if the magistrates should hear of
it they would be punished as murderers However,
the husband devised a scheme to get rid of the
corpse. He remembered that a Jewish doctor lived
just by, and having formed his plan, his wife and he
took the corpse, the one by the feet and the other
by the head, and carried it to the physician's house
They knocked at the door, from which a steep flight
of stairs led to his chamber. The servant-maid
came down without any light and, opening the door,
asked what they wanted. "Have the goodness," said
the tailor, "to go up again and tell your master we
have brought him a man who is very ill and wants
his advice. Here," continued he, putting a piece of
money into her hand, "give him that beforehand, to
convince him that we do not mean to impose."
When the servant had gone up to inform her master,
the tailor and his wife hastily conveyed the hunchback's body to the head of the stairs and, leaving it
there, hurried away.

In the meantime the maid told the doctor that
a man and a woman waited for him at the door,
desiring he would come down and look at a sick
man whom they had brought with them, and put

"I have killed the poor fellow who was brought to me to be cured."

the money she had received into his hand. The doctor was delighted at being paid beforehand; he thought he must needs have a good patient, and one who should not be neglected. "Bring a light," cried he to the maid, "follow me quickly." As he spoke, he hastily ran towards the head of the stairs without waiting for a light, and came against the corpse with so much violence that he precipitated it to the bottom, and had nearly fallen with it. "Bring me a light," he cried again, "quick, quick."

At last she brought one, and he went downstairs with her; but when he saw that what he had kicked down was a dead man he was very much frightened.

"Unhappy man that I am," said he, "why did I attempt to come without a light! I have killed the poor fellow who was brought to me to be cured: doubtless I am the cause of his death, I am ruined. Mercy on me, they will be here out of hand, and drag me out of my house for a murderer."

Notwithstanding the perplexity and confusion into which he was thrown, he had the precaution to shut his door, for fear anyone passing by should observe the accident of which he reckoned himself to be the author. He told his wife, who likewise exclaimed that they were ruined unless they could find a means to be rid of the body that very night

"If we harbour it till the morning we are lost,"
said she.

The doctor racked his brain in vain, he could
not think of any stratagem to relieve his embarrassment, but his wife, who was more fertile in invention,
said, "Let us carry the body to the terrace of our
house, and throw it down
the chimney of our Mussulman neighbour."

This Mussulman was one
of the sultan's purveyors for
furnishing oil, butter and
articles of a similar nature,
and had a storehouse where
the rats and mice made prodigious havoc.

The Jewish doctor ap-
proving the proposed ex-
pedient, his wife and he
took the little hunchback

*The doctor racked his brain
in vain*

up to the roof of the house and, fastening ropes
under his armpits, let him down the chimney into
the purveyor's chamber so dexterously that he stood
upright against the wall, as if he had been alive.
When they found he had reached the bottom they
pulled up the ropes, and left the body in that
position.

They were scarcely seated in their chamber
when the purveyor, who had just returned from a

wedding-feast, went into his room with a lanthorn
in his hand. He was not a little surprised to discover a man standing in his chimney; but being a
stout fellow, and taking him to be a thief, he took
up a stick, and, making straight for the hunchback,
"Ah!" said he, "I thought the rats and mice ate

The purveyor was surprised to discover a man standing in his chimney.

my butter and tallow; but it is you who come down
the chimney to rob me. However, I think you
will have no wish to come here again." Upon this
he attacked the hunchback and struck him several
times with his stick. The corpse fell down flat on
the ground, and the purveyor redoubled his blows.
But, observing that the body did not move, he

regarded it more nearly and perceived it to be
dead. "Wretched man that I am," said he, "what
have I done! I have killed a man; alas! I have
carried my revenge too far."

He stood pale and thunderstruck, he fancied
he already saw the officers come to drag him
to condign punishment, and could not tell what
to do.

But when he had recovered himself a little he
took the crooked body of the hunchback upon
his shoulders, and carried it to the end of the
street, where he placed it in an upright posture,
against a shop he then returned without once
looking behind him.

A few minutes before daybreak, a Christian
merchant who was very rich, and furnished the
sultan's palace with various articles, happened to
come in that direction on his way to the bath.
When he came to the end of the street he
passed by the shop where the hunchback's body
had been placed and happened to jostle against
it, when it fell upon his back. The merchant,
thinking he was attacked by a robber, knocked it
down, and, after redoubling his blows, cried out
"Thieves!"

The outcry alarmed the watch, who came up
immediately, and finding a Christian beating a
Mussulman asked him what reason he had to
abuse a Mussulman in that manner.

"He would have robbed me," replied the merchant, "and pounced upon me from behind in order to take me by the throat."

"If he did," said the watch, "you have revenged yourself sufficiently; come, get off him"

At the same time he stretched out his hand to help the little hunchback up, but observing that he was dead, "Oh!" said he, "is it thus that a Christian dares to assassinate a Mussulman?" So saying he laid hold of the Christian, and carried him to the house of the officer of the police, where he was kept till the judge was ready to examine him In the meantime, the more the Christian merchant reflected upon his adventure the less could he conceive how such slight blows of his fist could have killed the man.

The judge, having heard the report of the watch and viewed the body, interrogated the prisoner, who could not deny the crime, though he had not committed it. But the judge, considering the little hunchback belonged to the sultan, for he was one of his buffoons, would not put the Christian to death without higher authority. For this end he went to the palace and acquainted one of the sultan's officers with what had happened, and received this answer. "I have no mercy to show to a Christian who kills a Mussulman." Upon this the judge ordered the execution to take place, and sent criers all over the city to proclaim that they were about to put a Christian to death for killing a Mussulman.

The merchant was brought to the place of execution, and the executioner was about to do his duty, when the sultan's purveyor pushed through the crowd, calling to him to stop, for that the Christian had not committed the murder, but he himself had done it.

Upon that the officer who attended the execution began to question the purveyor, who told him every circumstance of his having killed the little hunchback, and how he had conveyed the body to the place where the Christian merchant had found it "You were about," added he, "to put to death an innocent person, for how can he be guilty of the death of a man who was dead before he touched him? It is enough for me to have killed a Mussulman, without loading my conscience with the death of a Christian who is not guilty."

The sultan's purveyor having publicly charged himself with the death of the little hunchback, the officer could do no less than execute justice on the merchant. "Let the Christian go," said he, "and execute this man in his stead, since it appears by his own confession that he is guilty" Thereupon the executioner released the merchant and seized the purveyor; but just as he was going to carry out the sentence he heard the voice of

the Jewish doctor, earnestly entreating him to suspend the execution, and make room for him to
approach.

When he appeared before the judge he said.
"My lord, this Mussulman you are going to execute is not guilty. I am the criminal Last night
a man and a woman, who are unknown to me,
came to my door with a sick man; my maid went
and opened it without a light, and received from
them a piece of money with a commission to
come and desire me, in their name, to step down
and look at the patient. While she was delivering
her message, they conveyed the sick person to
the stair-head, and disappeared, I went, without
waiting till my servant had lighted a candle, and
in the dark happened to stumble upon the sick
person and kick him downstairs. Alas! I soon
discovered he was dead, and it was the crooked
Mussulman whose death you are now about to
avenge. My wife and I took the body, and after
conveying it up to the roof of the purveyor, our
next neighbour, whom you were going to put to
death unjustly, let it down the chimney into his
chamber. The purveyor finding it in his house,
took the little man for a thief, and after beating
him concluded he had killed him. But that
it was not so you will be convinced by this my
deposition; I am the sole author of the murder;
and though it was committed undesignedly, I am

resolved to expiate my crime, that I may not have to charge myself with the deaths of two Mussulmen.

The chief justice being now persuaded that the Jewish doctor was the murderer, gave orders for the executioner to seize him and release the purveyor. Accordingly the doctor was about to be executed when the tailor appeared, crying to the executioner to hold his hand, and make room for him that he might come and make his confession to the chief judge. Room having been made, "My lord," said he, "you have narrowly escaped taking away the lives of three innocent persons; but if you will have the patience to hear me, I will discover to you the real murderer of the crookbacked man. If his death is to be expiated by another's, I must be the man Yesterday, towards the evening, as I was at work in my shop and was disposed to be merry, the little hunchback came to my door and sat down; he sang a little, and so I invited him to spend the evening at my house. He accepted the invitation and went in with me. We sat down to supper and I gave him a plate of fish; but in eating, a bone stuck in his throat, and though my wife and I did our utmost to relieve him, he died in a few minutes His death afflicted us extremely, and for fear of being charged with it, we carried the body to the Jewish doctor's house and knocked.

The maid came and opened the door; I desired her to go up again and ask her master to come down and give his advice to a sick person whom we had brought along with us, and withal, to encourage him, I charged her to give him a piece of money, which I put into her hand. When she was gone, I carried the hunchback upstairs, and

laid him upon the uppermost step, and then my wife and I made the best of our way home. The doctor accidentally threw the body downstairs and concluded himself to be the author of his death. This being the case, release the doctor and let me die in his stead."

The executioner was making ready.

The chief justice and all the spectators wondered at the strange events which had ensued upon the death of the little hunchback. "Let the Jewish doctor go," said the judge, "and seize the tailor, since he confesses the crime."

While the executioner was making ready to put an end to the tailor, the Sultan of Caspar, wanting the company of his crooked jester, asked where he was. One of his officers replied that he

had been found dead in the city, and the most
strange circumstance about the death was that a
Christian merchant, the sultan's own purveyor, a
Jewish doctor and a tailor had all charged themselves in turn with the crime.

Upon receiving this intelligence the sultan sent
an officer to the place of execution. "Go," said
he, "with all expedition, and tell the judge to
bring the accused persons before me immediately,
and bring also the body of my poor hunchback
that I may see him once more."

Accordingly the officer went, and happened to
arrive at the place of execution at the very time
that the executioner had laid his hands upon the
tailor. He called to him to suspend the execution,
and acquainted the judge with the sultan's pleasure.
The judge obeyed, and went directly to the palace,
accompanied by the tailor, the Jewish doctor, the
purveyor and the Christian merchant, and four men
conveyed the body of the hunchback along with
them.

When they appeared in the sultan's presence,
the judge threw himself at the prince's feet, and
afterwards gave him a faithful record of all that
had happened.

The story appeared most extraordinary to the
sultan, and addressing himself to the audience, he
said. "Did you ever hear such a surprising event
as has happened to my little crooked buffoon?"

Now there was present a barber who had listened very attentively to the story of the little hunchback, and who now asked leave to examine the body a little nearer.

This being granted, he approached him, sat down on the ground, took his head between his knees, and after he had looked upon him steadfastly, fell into so great a fit of laughter and had so little command of himself that he fell backwards on the ground, without considering that he was before the Sultan of Caspar.

"Barber," said the sultan, "why do you laugh?"

"Sir," answered the barber, "I swear by your Majesty's benevolence that the hunchback is not dead, and I shall be content to pass for a dotard if I do not convince you of it this minute."

So saying, he took a box wherein he had several medicines that he carried about him to use as occasion might require, and drew out a little phial of balsam, with which he rubbed the hunchback's neck a long time; then he took out of his case a neat iron instrument which he inserted between the hunchback's teeth, and after he had opened his mouth, he thrust a pair of small pincers down his throat, with which he drew out a fish bone. Immediately the hunchback sneezed, stretched forth his arms and feet, opened his eyes, and showed several other signs of life.

The sultan was transported with joy and ad-

Lightning Source UK Ltd.
Milton Keynes UK
UKHW010827160223
417122UK00011B/1096

9 781017 698701

The Arabian Nights.